BRAHMS

and his

WOMEN'S CHORUSES

By

SOPHIE DRINKER, Mus.D.

1952

Published by
SOPHIE DRINKER
249 Merion Rd.,
Merion, Pa.

Under the Auspices of
MUSURGIA PUBLISHERS
Dr. Albert G. Hess

BRAHMS
and his
WOMEN'S CHORUSES

ILLUSTRATIONS

PREFACE

A study dealing thoroughly with the women's chorus, which Johannes Brahms founded in Hamburg, has been long overdue. In full-size biographies this episode is more or less passed over. Yet it was of the utmost importance for the development of young Brahms. Decisive features of his artistic personality were first revealed in the work he did through three years with this enthusiastic group. His peculiar technique in writing for vocal ensembles, his interest in the skillful combination of womens voices, his deep love for the folksong found expression in his compositions and arrangements for the little chorus. The girls' delighted response meant encouragement, their willingness to follow him on new paths gave him a testing ground so important for a young composer.

Sophie Drinker, who has made it her lifetask to study the position of women in various cultural fields, and especially in music, is singularly qualified for her work. She collected pertinent data with the greatest energy and devotion and succeeded in unearthing a great deal of unknown and attractive material. Out of it emerges a charming picture of a group of music-minded young ladies in the middle of the past century and of their adored leader, the young genius, who was still looking at the future with glowing confidence, blissfully ignorant of the fact that there was to be no place for him in his native city, where he was confident that he had established an important foothold through his work with the women's chorus.

Karl and Irene Geiringer

Boston, May 1951.

Laura Garbe, Betty Völckers, Marie Reuter,
Marie Völckers formed the far-famed vocal
quartette which evolved from the
Hamburger Frauenchor (see p. 59).

I

THE SOURCE MATERIAL
AND BIBLIOGRAPHY

Brahms was thirty years old in 1863 and, before then, he had worked for several years with women's choruses. All of his biographers mention these groups for which he composed the lovely music we still enjoy. But no one of the authors gives all the available data nor do they entirely agree on many points of interest, especially on the history of the *Hamburger Frauenchor*.

The purpose of this little book is to bring the original sources of information together in chronological order.

The unpublished material consists of:

1. Extracts from the Diary of Franziska Meier, a member of the *Hamburger Frauenchor*, as copied out by Anna Lentz, her daughter, from her original manuscript.

2. Letters from Anna Lentz.

3. Memoirs of Friedchen Wagner, the founder of the *Hamburger Frauenchor*, as sent by her son, Kurt Sauermann.

4. Letters from Hans Albrecht, who assisted me in collecting the material.

5. Letters from Karl Geiringer, Curator of the Museum of the *Gesellschaft der Musikfreunde*, Vienna, in 1937.

6. The *Stimmenhefte* (music note-books) made by the singers, who copied out their individual voice parts from Brahms' manuscripts.

The *Stimmenhefte* referred to here belonged to Friedchen Wagner, Franziska and Camilla Meier, Marie and Betty Völckers, all members of the *Hamburger Frauenchor*.

These books contain:

I   Twenty-five compositions subsequently published for women's voices;

II   Seven original songs subsequently arranged by Brahms for mixed chorus or for solo voice;

III   One original part song for women's voices, arranged by Brahms from the solo song, Op. 14, No. 8;

IV   One original part song for women's voices, transposed by Brahms from his setting for men's voices, later published as Op. 41, No. 1;

V   Two canons not published in Brahms' lifetime;

VI   A short original part song, not published in Brahms' lifetime;

VII   Two unfinished compositions;

VIII Fifty-five folk songs in 3 or 4 parts, some in both;

IX   Thirty-two pieces by other composers;

X   Twelve songs and canons in Brahms' manuscript. (App. E)

(See Appendix for detailed lists)

I have five of Friedchen's note-books. Four of them contain the single voice parts of some of the music sung by the chorus. In her "Stimme 1" book is Vineta, written out by her with corrections and alterations in Brahms' own hand. The fifth of the little, thin, brown volumes is the *Partitur der Volkslieder*. In it is the piano accompaniment to *Der Gärtner* (Op. 17, No. 3). On the title page, with a list of songs, are the words: *Brahms, dreistimmig, gesetzt für uns.* "Brahms, three part, set for us" can mean only one thing: that Brahms made three part settings of folksongs for Friedchen and her friends and that the songs are inscribed in this note-book.

According to Anna Lentz, Franziska Meier's tiny note-
books containing only her own part were the ones she sang
from at the weekly meetings of the *Hamburger Frauenchor*.
Later, she and her sister Camilla made the larger books with
all the parts, including piano accompaniments to Nos. 2, 3,
and 4 of Op. 17. Franziska drew the charming illustrations
that reveal so much of fact and fancy in the lives of these
musically talented girls. (See Chapter IX)

The ten books of the Völckers sisters are especially
valuable, since they contain what is undoubtedly the complete
second soprano and alto parts of the unfinished *Benedictus*
and *Brautgesang*. (See Chapter III) I do not have the volume
with the soprano solo and a few bars of the soprano tutti of
the Brautgesang, evidently the only one seen by Kalbeck and
described by him in Vol. I, 2, p. 376 of his *Johannes Brahms*.
Best of all, in the Völckers' books, are twelve songs written
out by Brahms himself, three of which are reproduced in this
study. (See Appendix E)

My interest in Brahms' music for women was aroused by a
women's chorus which met in our music room at Merion, Pennsylvania, for about fifteen years. As I sang a second alto
part in that compelling Romantic music, I used to wonder
what those girls, who had first sung it, were like and what
were the circumstances that had led Brahms to compose it.

The enthusiasm of the Montgomery Singers was shared and,
in fact, enhanced by the interest of my husband, Henry S.
Drinker. At that time, he was translating the vocal texts
of Brahms, both the solo songs and the choral works. His
editions, with English words, of compositions previously
published and of other works originally written for the
Hamburger Frauenchor added to our repertoire and to our
enjoyment. His complete edition of Brahms' compositions for
women's voices is listed in Appendix D.

At this same time - 1934 - my husband and I became friends with Etta Albrecht, a German girl from Hamburg and a student at Bryn Mawr College. We often talked to her about Brahms and Hamburg and wondered if we could find out something about the young women of the *Frauenchor*. We wished, too, to trace the *Stimmenhefte*, the music note-books into which the singers had copied their individual parts from Brahms' manuscripts.

Etta suggested that we ask her father, Dr. Hans Albrecht, to make inquiries in Hamburg. His interest in our project, his industry in following every lead that might be rewarding for our research, and his tact in persuading the families of the *Frauenchor* members to share their treasures with us far exceeded our expectations.

His first success was the acquisition of Franziska and Camilla Meier's books that were then in the possession of Anna Lentz, Franziska's daughter. When my husband went to Hamburg in 1935, Dr. Albrecht introduced him to Anna. She interpreted for him the sketches drawn by her mother and gave us Franziska's diary as edited in the *Jahrbuch der Gesellschaft Hamburger Kunstfreunde, 1902*. A copy of the *Jahrbuch* is in my possession. Later, she copied out other unpublished extracts referring to the *Frauenchor*.

The version of the Diary which follows here, pp. 24-41, is the result first of translating the extracts published in the *Jahrbuch der Gesellschaft Hamburger Kunstfreunde, 1902*, and the additional extracts copied out by Anna Lentz in 1935, and second by piecing the two together as they must have been in the original. Franziska often wrote incomplete sentences which, in the translation, have been made grammatical to simplify reading. She frequently refers to matters about which there is no other information. But wherever possible, explanations of puzzling references have been inserted between the passages quoted from the Diary.

We kept up a correspondence with Anna until her death in 1939 and will always remember the kind old lady who used the money we paid for the *Stimmenhefte* to buy her nephew a good violin.

We were particularly pleased when Dr. Albrecht discovered Friedchen Wagner's son, Kurt Sauermann, the owner of a small bookstore in Hamburg. Kurt had a trunkful of his mother's papers in his attic. He was willing to sell us her *Stimmenhefte* and a charming photograph. He wrote us some of his own recollections of Brahms and sent us a copy of his mother's memoirs, in so far as they referred to the women's chorus and to her friendship with Brahms. Kurt Sauermann is now dead and his family possessions were destroyed during the Second World War. But from the papers of the Sauermanns which are here, the real origin of the *Hamburger Frauenchor* can be understood.

The following year, Dr. Albrecht went to Bonn to interview Frau Clara von Königslow, the daughter-in-law of Betty Völckers. Being unwilling to sell the *Stimmenhefte* in her possession outside of Germany, the family kindly allowed photostats to be made of them for us. Frau von Königslow gave Dr. Albrecht a picture of the old Völckers house in Hamburg where the *Frauenchor* often met and also several photographs of the singers. (See pp. 69 and 44). In June 1951, I wrote to Frau von Königslow to ask her again to let us have the *Stimmenhefte* containing the Brahms' manuscripts. The answer was that her books and papers had all been destroyed by floods of water in the basement during the war. This unfortunate fact, however, obviously enhances the value of our photostats.

The *Stimmenhefte* were known to Kalbeck, Hübbe, Florence May, and probably to the other biographers. Kalbeck and Hübbe inspected them and both did some classification of the contents. But even Hübbe's list is not complete. The books we have contain more music than he mentions. And since they correspond to each other down to the smallest detail, the authenticity of the music written in them is unquestionable. From the different volumes, the vocal parts of most of the unpublished compositions can be reconstructed. Other books, not yet located, or permanently lost, must have had the voice parts of the Psalm, Op. 27, and five of the *Marienlieder*, known from diaries and letters to have been sung by the *Hamburger Frauenchor*.

From the time the chorus disbanded in 1863, the *Stimmenhefte* remained in private hands. At present, they are in our library at Merion, Pennsylvania. Eventually, they will go to the Smith College Library at Northampton, Massachusetts, with the entire correspondence between us and our German friends.

As far as the other women's choruses are concerned, the information about Göttingen is in E. Michelmann's book *Agathe von Siebold*. About Vienna, no account of women's activities in choral singing that I know of exists. For the details of my knowledge, I am indebted to Karl Geiringer who, during the years 1937 and 1938, kindly wrote me voluminous letters in answer to my queries. The correspondence with him opened my eyes to the apparently unappreciated extent to which women's choruses functioned in the musical life of Germany up to the time of the First World War. Familiarity with this particular aspect of women's participation in music gave me a new perspective on Brahms' association with women's choruses and helped me to integrate the accounts of the *Hamburger Frauenchor* and the von Asten's chorus with the other events in his career.

The published material which I have drawn upon is as follows:

J. Brahms, *Briefwechsel* (Berlin: Deutsche Brahms Gesellschaft, 1907-22). 16 Vols.

H. S. Drinker, *Texts of the Vocal Works of Johannes Brahms in English Translation*, 1945. (Apply to Association of American Choruses, c/o Westminster Choir College, Princeton, N. J.)

Sophie Drinker, "Brahms' Music for Women", *Music Clubs Magazine*, Nov.-Dec. 1939 and Jan. 1940.

Music and Women (New York: Coward-McCann, Inc., 1948.)

A. von Ehrmann, *Johannes Brahms: Thematisches Verzeichniss Seiner Werk* (Leipsig: Breitkopf und Härtel, 1933.)

M. Friedländer, *Brahms' Lieder* (London: Oxford University Press, 1928)

K. Geiringer, *Brahms, His Life and Work*, 2nd Edition (New York: Oxford University Press, 1947)

"Johannes Brahms im Briefwechsel mit E. Mandyczewski", *Zeitschrift für Musikwissenschaft*, 1933.

W. Hübbe, *Brahms in Hamburg* (Hamburg: Gesellschaft Hamburgischer Kunstfreunde, 1902)

M. Kalbeck, *Johannes Brahms* (Berlin: Deutsche Brahms Gesellschaft, 1904-14)

A. Kretschmer and W. von A. Zuccalmaglio, *Deutsche Volkslieder mit ihren Original Weisen*, 2 Vols. (Berlin, 1840)

B. Litzmann, *Clara Schumann, An Artist's Life* (London: Macmillan and Co., 1913) 2 Vols.

Letters of Clara Schumann and Johannes Brahms (London: Edward Arnold, 1927)

Florence May, *Johannes Brahms* (London: Edward Arnold, 1905)

Franziska Meier, "Diary", *Jahrbuch der Gesellschaft Hamburger Kunstfreunde* (Hamburg, 1902)

E. Michelmann, *Agathe von Siebold* (Stuttgart und Berlin: J. G. Cotta'sche Buchhandlung Nachfolger, 1930)

W. Niemann, *Brahms* (New York: Alfred A. Knopf, 1929, translated by Catherine A. Phillip)

G. Ophüls, *Brahms' Texte* (Berlin: N. Simrock, 1898)

Susanne Schmaltz, *Beglückte Errinerungen* (Germany) Extracts sent by Kurt Sauermann

I am indebted to these publishers for their permission to quote passages from biographies of Brahms:

Oxford University Press, *Brahms' Lieder* by M. Friedländer.

The Macmillan Company, *Clara Schumann* by B. Litzmann.

Edward Arnold and Co., *Letters of Clara Schumann & Johannes Brahms*, compiled by B. Litzmann.

William Reeves (new edition), *Johannes Brahms* by Florence May.

Alfred A. Knopf, *Brahms*, by W. Niemann.

But especially my hearty thanks are due to both Karl and Irene Geiringer for their friendly encouragement and their invaluable suggestions on the final draft of "Brahms and His Women's Choruses".

SOPHIE DRINKER
Merion, Pa.
1951

II

THE ORIGIN OF THE
HAMBURGER FRAUENCHOR 1856-58

"Friedchen Wagner is the principal founder of my Verein here
and we sing at her house ..."

So Brahms wrote to tell Clara Schumann that "his favorite
pupil" was going with her father to Wildbad, where Clara was
taking the cure.

In this same letter, dated July 3, 1859, Brahms went on
to say:

"You have already met her here (Hamburg) and, if you feel the
least inclination to do so, you ought to see her there. She
is an exceedingly charming, modest, and musical girl and
ought to please you ..." [1]

Brahms himself had been pleased with Friedchen since
1855. At that time, he was twenty-two years old. She was
twenty, small and not pretty, but full of fire and high
spirits. Her passionate temperament found an outlet in music
and endeared her to Clara as well as to Brahms. Her piano
playing also delighted Brahms, who remarked upon her ability
in the same letter:

"Incidentally, she plays quite well and can do all kinds of
things with her little fingers."

In 1855, Friedchen was taking piano lessons from her
cousin G. D. Otten. One evening, at his house on the Linden-
strasse in Hamburg, while she was playing duets with him she
met Brahms.

"I saw Brahms for the first time one evening at Otten's, just
as I was playing Schubert's Divertissements for four hands
with him. When Brahms appeared in the doorway, I wanted to
stop playing but Otten wished us to play the piece to the
end which proved very profitable for me, since Brahms im-

Friedchen Wagner, 1831-1917; married Kurt Sauerman
in 1869. When this photograph was taken in 1865,
she was thirty-four years old.

mediately said that he himself wanted to play it over again
with me.

"After supper he offered to take me home. On the way, I
asked him to give me lessons twice a week. So the instruction
began. I had been technically prepared by my dear Mr. Avé.
It was thanks to his efforts that Brahms took such kind
interest in my playing from the very beginning, a fact which
he later expressed in a letter to Frau Schumann when she was
in Wildbad.

"My instruction continued with a short interruption while
Brahms was in Detmold. Brahms often played with me (Mozart
and Händel) and through him, I became acquainted with Bach
(Well-Tempered Clavier). Through his excellent fingering, I
mastered the technical difficulties relatively easily. Later,
he often played his compositions with me (for four hands).
Frau Schumann, who also came to my parents', visited Brahms
frequently. While my piano was being repaired at Heins' in
the Pferdemarkt, I had my lessons in Heins' piano store at
5 o'clock in the afternoon. After the lesson, Brahms gave
me the pleasure of playing for me. We often played Bach's
Concerto for three pianos; his brother Fritz participating.
Once, however, I played at Heins' with Brahms and Clara
Schumann. It was at Brahms' suggestion. I was nervous and
lost my place. Frau Schumann encouraged me. We were able
to continue and it went off all right. Frau Schumann said
that such a thing could happen to anybody. In playing the
third piano in Bach's Concerto, I had to count twenty-three
bars rest!" [2]

Friedchen's family belonged to the upper middle class.
As a group, these people were both industrious and prosperous,
spending much of their leisure time in cultivating the arts.
They sang part songs and played instruments at home. They
founded choral societies by the score. Their familiarity
with musical terms and idioms enabled them to appreciate the
skill of professional performers and to understand contemporary composition. With their informal music and public
concerts, they made Germany the Mecca of musicians the world
over.

Friedchen lived with her parents and her two sisters,
Thusnelda and Olga, on Pastorenstrasse. Brahms was a frequent

visitor at the Wagner's house. Besides giving the musically intelligent girl her piano lessons, he played for her and, above all, talked with her.

At that time Brahms was steeping himself in the rich treasures of German folksong, sharing with other scholars a vivid interest in the old songs, as well as in those of contemporary origin. At the same time, informal singing by truly musical people was an entertainment that had no competition with mechanically made music. It was so popular a game that it challenged the attention of those with a talent for invention. Brahms had already dedicated a set of songs to the Schumann children and was busy making piano accompaniments to others. And his interest was more than a youthful enthusiasm for he never lost sight of the musical value of the folksong nor of the social value of home singing. At the end of his life, he compiled a volume of 49 Folksongs and composed such inimitable piano accompaniments to them that no one could doubt his respect for the original material.

In Friedchen's Memoirs, she reported her reaction to her conversations with Brahms about his favorite folksongs:

> "While I was taking lessons from Brahms, I asked him one morning -- since my two sisters and I often sang together -- to compose folksongs for that purpose, which he was very willing to do."

Friedchen gives no date but Hübbe attributes her request to the summer and autumn of 1856.

The songs that Brahms first offered the girls may have been some of the *28 Deutsche Volkslieder* for solo with piano accompaniment. He was working on this set between 1854 and 1858. Those arranged for three women's voices from this set are:

Der Bucklichte Fiedler (Es wohnet ein Fiedler)
Trennung (Da unten im Tale)

Gang zur Liebsten (Des Abends kann ich nicht schlafen gehen)

Der Zimmergesell (Es war einmal)

Drei Vöglein (Mit Lust thät ich ausreiten)

Gunhilde

Der Todte Gast (Es pocket ein Knabe)

Altes Minnelied (Ich fahr dahin)

Die Versuchung (Feinsliebchen, du sollst)

Die Wollust in den Maien

Friedchen continued the story in her Memoirs but still without a definite date:

"After a short time, several young ladies came to take part in the singing and thus gradually a women's chorus was formed in my parents' house."

The authentic account of the beginning of the *Hamburger Frauenchor* thus occurs in two sources which correspond: Brahms' letter of July 3, 1859, to Clara Schumann and Friedchen Wagner's Memoirs. At first, Friedchen sang folksongs arranged by Brahms with Thusnelda and Olga. Then, she invited other young women ... probably one or two at a time, possibly different ones on different evenings ... until circumstances drew many more music lovers into the original intimate group.

Johannes Brahms, as he looked at the
time of the founding of the
Hamburger Frauenchor.

III
THE INFLUENCE OF GÖTTINGEN
1858

During the late 50s, Brahms did not stay in Hamburg all the time but travelled around Germany on business or pleasure.

In June, 1858, he was invited by his friend, Julius Otto Grimm, the popular founder and leader of the *Cäcilia Verein* in Göttingen, to come there for the summer. Grimm well knew what appeal to make. Clara Schumann would be there. Brahms would find an organ to play on and, best of all, singing.

> "If it would please you to have a few good voices, lodged in very lovely girls, sing for you, they will take pleasure in being at your disposal. Come now quickly!" [3]

Brahms decided to accept the invitation and found that Göttingen offered more than he had anticipated. One of the lovely girls in Göttingen was Philippine, Grimm's wife, nicknamed Pine Gur, on account of the gutteral way she pronounced the letter R. Daughter of the piano manufacturer Ritmüller, she was a brilliant pianist herself as well as a good choral singer. Another singer was Agathe von Siebold, with whom Brahms fell in love, and she with him. All summer long, they sang and played together.

Brahms' songs in Op. 14 and Op. 19 belong to this period, inspired by Agathe and her beautiful soprano voice. The duets of Op. 20, Nos. 1 and 2, composed in September, 1858, were sung by Agathe and her friend Bertha Wagner, whose wonderfully rich alto voice also delighted Brahms.

Philippine, Agathe, Bertha, and other young women belonged to the *Cäcilia Verein*, Grimm's chorus of ninety members. They also sang in a women's chorus. For both groups, Grimm wrote music. He loved to compose and, in his day, it was quite customary for conductors to perform their own compositions. His style was post-Mendelssohnian and, although he was a most prolific composer, none of his music has survived on modern programmes. His devoted women friends, however, no doubt sang it with zest, especially a set of old Low German poems, called by Grimm, *Ein Liederkranz*.

When Brahms arrived, these choruses were in full swing. Fresh from his Hamburg circle of girls, he looked with interest upon those of Göttingen. His musical ingenuity was challenged and he was eager to experiment with women's voices. One composition was a *Benedictus* from a Mass upon which he had been working in 1856. Unfortunately for the choral literature of women, he did not finish the *Benedictus*. Its canon was used later in the Motet Op. 74; *Warum ist das Licht*.

Another trial composition was a *Brautgesang* (Bridal Song) for soprano solo and women's chorus. The words are Uhland's:

> *Das Haus benedei'ich und preis es laut.*
> "I bless the house that has received a beautiful bride and praise it. Into a garden it must blossom."

For some unknown reason, the *Brautgesang* missed fire. It was evidently basically inferior, pronounced so by his two friends, Clara and Grimm.

Clara expressed her disapproval:

> "I like certain parts of the *Brautgesang* very much -- the last bar on p. 15 is wonderful. But it has struck me that here and there the motifs are a little bit commonplace -- I should have thought of Hiller, or some other musician, and not of you -- Forgive me, I dare say what I have said is silly, but every time I played the piece through, I felt this more and more." [4]

And in writing after Brahms had left for Detmold, Grimm was at first non-committal:

> "I could not send the *Brautgesang* back yesterday because I only received it this afternoon. I had to read it through and play it to the ladies Gathe and Gur. That has been done and they think it is glorious, delightful, refreshing, and so on. I, too. But the two songs of Uhland's, Op. 19, Nos. 2 and 3, *(Scheiden und Meiden; In der Ferne)* have so moved me that, at the moment, there is no place left for the *Brautgesang*. Both words and music in those songs are too moving to allow me to enter the blessed house in a congenial mood. I will be glad when Gathe can sing them properly ..."

Another letter is more forceful:

> "Your *Brautgesang* did not please me so much (as the *Grabgesang*). I am not being silent about anything. I will not presume hastily and impudently to approach it." [5]

Brahms answered from Detmold:

> "Thank you for your criticisms ... The *Brautlied* is disgracefully ordinary and dull. The poem could be beautifully composed. As it is, a poor composer sits sadly and alone in his room and conjures up thoughts which are none of his business. And a critic sets himself between two beautiful ladies ... I don't want to picture it any further!" [5]

Brahms could not have been entirely convinced that the *Brautlied* was "disgracefully ordinary and dull" or he would not have allowed the voice parts to be copied out later into the *Stimmenhefte* of the *Hamburger Frauenchor*. Although no mention of its performance or even of its practice is made in the diaries or letters at hand, the *Brautlied* must have been sung in Hamburg between 1859 and 1862. But Brahms eventually abandoned it as a choral composition for women's voices and used the melody in his magnificent song *von Ewiger Liebe*. (See p. 70)

In spite of the failure of the *Brautgesang*, the experience at Göttingen deepened Brahms' perception of the potentialities of a women's chorus. While there, he came in contact with a large and well-trained group of women. He immediately conceived original compositions for them, compositions which were in a different musical category from the simple folksongs he had set for the Hamburg girls.

His next attempt had a happier fate. The *Ave Maria*, Op. 12, was a success from its conception at Göttingen in September, 1858. The text is the liturgical invocation to the Virgin Mary.

> *Ave Maria, gratia plena, Dominus te cum, benedicta tu in mulieribus, et benedictus fructus ventris tui, Jesus. Sancta Maria! Ora pro nobis!*

Brahms broke many precedents by clothing these words in a romantic idiom and by offering the composition to a choir of laywomen. His inspiration to do so may have come partly from the sight of wayside shrines with peasant women kneeling and offering flowers to the Virgin. But it was certainly the spirit of Agathe herself, a Catholic with an understanding of the religious text, that ultimately kindled his imagination.

The original version had an organ accompaniment, as if it were intended for church use by a women's choir. Whether the Göttingen girls sang it before Brahms left for Detmold at the end of September 1858 is at present unknown, but might be disclosed in forgotten letters or diaries of members of the chorus. (Appendix F)

Although Grimm's chorus was in no sense under Brahms' leadership, it must be included in any account of his association with a women's chorus since it provided him with the incentive that started his serious work for soprano and alto voices.

In Detmold, where he conducted the choral society at the castle, he lost no time in giving his new *Ave Maria* publicity in the court circle. He asked the Princess

Frederica and the other women members of the *Schloss-Chor* to sing his compositions for women's voices, offering them both the three-part folksongs and the *Ave Maria*. Then, encouraged by their enthusiasm, he carried the manuscript with him to Hamburg when he returned home at the end of January, 1859.

Joachim conducting the Brahms Serenade,
op. 11, March 26, 1859.
Sketch by Franziska Meier.

Brahms conducting his 2nd Serenade,
op. 16, March 28, 1860.
Sketch by Franziska Meier.
It is interesting that Brahms appears here
with spectacles on, since the fact that he
wore them has not been remarked by others.

IV
DEVELOPMENTS IN HAMBURG
1859

Like most German cities, Hamburg supported several choruses. One of them was the *Hamburg Akademie*, directed by Karl Grädener. According to the custom of the times, the women members often sang without the men, especially to perform music composed by Grädener himself.

One day, in April, 1859, Grädener inquired whether the chorus would like to sing a composition by Brahms. "Fräulein Gobbin and the whole alto section rose in assent", wrote Franziska Meier in her diary.

The enthusiastic response suggests that these young women already knew Brahms or had heard favorably of him. Probably most of them had attended the concert in March when the Serenade, Op. 11, was played, Joachim conducting. Franziska was there and recorded the sentiments of at least some of the concert-going public. Her diary of March is filled with details of how she and her friends haunted Wörmer's Hall for the rehearsals and the performance of the Serenade. After the concert, her excitement was intense and compelled her to make pen and ink drawings of the musicians. The following entry refers to this memorable event:

> "March 29. I spent an almost sleepless night during which I wrote in my diary, made poetry and drew sketches of Joachim and Brahms."

Although somewhat crudely executed, these sketches are authentic and genuine impressions of the two artists.

Some of the members of Grädener's chorus probably knew Friedchen and might have been accustomed to sing with the

Karl Grädener, conductor of the *Hamburg Akademie,*
an institution which existed from 1851 to 1867.
He composed for the women members
of that chorus.

Wagner sisters. It seems practically certain that the girls
were singing the three-part folksongs arranged for them by
Brahms during the spring of 1859. Brahms was in Hamburg then;
Friedchen was studying piano with him. And above all, it was
to Friedchen that Brahms turned for advice when an opportunity arose for him to hear his *Ave Maria* again.

One of Grädener's pupils, Jenny von Ahsen, was married
on May 19 in St. Michael's Church. Brahms played the organ
at the wedding and Grädener conducted his girl choir in the
singing of a motet he had composed for the occasion. The
text was taken from the Bible; Psalm 127:

> "Except the Lord build the house, they labour in vain who
> build it."

It was set for four parts and the fourth voice had the cantus
firmus, which was the old melody so often used by Bach, the
famous *Morgenstern Chorale (Wie schön leuchtet der Morgenstern)*.
Although Grädener's composition has disappeared from the
catalogues, it was well received at the time and was performed later by Brahms in a church concert. (See p. 40)

Brahms was so favorably impressed with the singing and
with the general effect of the women's voices in the church
that he immediately conceived the idea of creating an occasion for the performance of his own *Ave Maria* and of composing more music to religious texts for women's voices.
Since he was engrossed at the time in studying Palestrina
and other masters of the a capella school, he wrote two four
part motets in the 16th century style. The first was *O Bone
Jesu* and the second, *Adoramus*. These were later published
as Nos. 1 and 2 of Op. 37.

Brahms apparently appealed to Friedchen for help in
organizing a group to sing his music. She responded by in-
viting a number of singers to her house. Among them, un-

doubtedly, were her own friends and Grädener's chorus of the girls who had performed at the wedding.

On Monday, June 6, twenty-eight volunteers turned up at the Wagner's house. Brahms conducted them in singing. A lady, whose name Hübbe does not give, told him that they sang "a quite beautiful *Ave Maria* to which Avé listened with open mouth and was filled with rapture." [6]

O Bone Jesu and *Adoramus* were also practiced. These seemed to the lady who was Hübbe's informant very difficult and not so pleasing. Grädener, too, was at the rehearsal and evidently helped Brahms through a fit of embarrassment which seized him as he confronted the new group. The next morning, however, the programme was repeated. On June 8 the chorus went to St. Peter's Church and sang the *Ave Maria* and the two motets there.

Encouraged by the enthusiasm of the chorus and eager to make the most of the opportunity for composition, Brahms asked the young women to sing with him once a week. Two of the singers were Marie and Betty Völckers. Many years later, Marie told Kalbeck:

> "My elder sister Betty belonged to a singing society and, as so often happened, several ladies of the chorus were asked to sing at a wedding in the church; it was under the direction of Grädener. Brahms played the organ and, after the ceremony, he asked the ladies if they would like to sing some songs composed by him. The proposal was accepted with enthusiasm and regular rehearsals were arranged in the mornings. From that originated the *Frauenchor*." [7]

Either Marie had not been intimate with the Wagners or, if she had sung informally of an evening with the three sisters, she did not regard a small group of girls singing part songs for fun as a *Frauenchor*. After the wedding, Brahms made a definite engagement to be present at meetings himself, promising not only to conduct but to supply the chorus with compositions that could be performed before an audience. He even invented a motto for them. FIX ODER NIX, Up to the Mark or Nothing. The *formal* organization of the *Frauenchor* took place then.

On June 20, Brahms brought a novelty for the chorus ... two *Marienlieder*. These are songs in which the Virgin Mary is heroine in all kinds of imaginary adventures. German literature is full of them, a great many poets and musicians having contributed to their making. Before 1858, Brahms himself harmonized one, *Der englische Gruss*, which appears now as No. 8 of the *28 Deutsche Volkslieder* for One Voice and Piano Accompaniment. It is the angel's greeting to Mary, the Annunciation. But the composition he offered the women's chorus was original, his own melody.

Brahms' appreciation that this type of song would be attractive material for a women's chorus resulted in the composition of six Marienlieder for two soprano and two alto voices. When writing later to the publisher Simrock, he explained how he used the folkpoems but made his own music:

"The poems are all beautiful folksongs and the music somewhat in the manner of the old church music and folksong." [8]

The two that he brought to the rehearsal on June 20 were *Der englische Gruss* and *Maria's Kirchgang*. The second of these is in Franziska Lentz' book, *Versammlung 3*, written a whole tone higher throughout than Brahms' published edition of the Marienlieder for mixed voices, Op. 22. It is the only one that appears in the *Stimmenhefte*.

When Mary once to church would go
She fain would cross a deep, wide sea.
And as she reached the waters' flow
A boatman there she chanced to see.
"Oh boatman safely ferry thou me,
What e'er thou ask I'll give to thee."
"I'll bear thee safely over the sea,
If thou wilt come and marry me."

Marienlied, No. 2, in the original key as composed for the
Hamburger Frauenchor. From Franziska Lentz' Stimmenheft,
marked Versammlung No. 3.

"Before I deign to marry thee,
I'll swim alone across the sea."
Now as she neared the other side,
All the church bells ringing out far and wide,
Both large and small, with one accord,
Proclaimed the Mother of our Lord.
And when the shore they did regain,
The boat-man's heart was broke in twain.

In the musical treatment of this poem, Brahms gave the melody to the first altos and, where the text refers to the church bells, he had the voices reproduce the sound of bells ringing by repeating over and over the intervals of fourths and fifths. (See Appendix D)

Unfortunately, the Stimmenhefte containing the other *Marienlieder* later sung by the Frauenchor are still missing. But in several of the books is one by Johann Eccard, a 16th century composer.

> *Uber's Gebirge Maria geht*
> Over the mountain goes Mary

This had previously been copied out by Brahms into his 1854 notebook. At some point in the Frauenchor's history, Brahms transposed it from the setting for S. S. A. T. B. up a major third to arrange it comfortably for the range of S. S. A. A. A. (See Appendix D)

The young women's enthusiasm for the choral singing was equalled by that of Brahms. He mentioned the chorus to three friends with whom he corresponded during the summer. In answer to one of his letters, Clara Schumann wrote:

> "How delightful about your *Gesangverein*. I hope you have a large number of charming girls in it. But don't you include men as well? I should think you would soon find women's singing alone monotonous. I should like to hear your songs. How did you like the songs which you tried with the organ on June 9? Aren't they very difficult? Did your girls sing them well?" [9]

But Brahms did not find women's voices monotonous. Nor

Théodor Avé-Lallement, a music teacher and
member of the committee for the Philharmonic
concerts. He and Brahms were
intimate friends.

did Avé and Grädener, who both attended most of the rehearsals.

In August, Brahms alluded to the *Frauenchor* again when writing to Joachim:

> "A little singing society (ladies only) detains me. Otherwise, I would have been on the Rhine or in some beautiful forest." [10]

And a little later, he offered Fräulein von Meysenbug, one of the singers in the castle chorus at Detmold, two explanations of his interest in the women's voices:

> "I am here and shall probably remain until I go to Detmold. Some very pleasant pupils detain me and, strangely enough, a ladies' society that sings under my direction, till now only what I compose for it. The clear, silver tones please me exceedingly and, in the church with the organ, the ladies' voices sound quite charming." [11]

Franziska Meier in 1861

V

FRANZISKA MEIER'S DIARY
1859

Franziska Meier was twenty-three years old in the summer of 1859. She came from the same type of upper middleclass family as Friedchen Wagner. Her mother, Frau Senatorin Meier, served as a member of the committee of Grund's Academy, a concert-giving institution. Her sister Camilla, aged twenty-one, played the piano and sang in the mixed chorus of the Cäcilia Verein, conducted by Dr. Spengel.

Franziska herself was a girl with a talent for sketching, making poetry and music. (See illustrations, p. 79) She studied both voice and piano and attended concerts enthusiastically. Her special companions were her sister Camilla and Susanne Schmaltz. They called themselves "The Three Crows". (See p. 79) From Susanne's book, *Beglückte Erinnerungen*, and from entries in Franziska's diary of March and April, 1859, the girls' sentimental adoration of Joachim and Brahms as musical heroes is revealed. (See Chap. IV) In view of this, it is surprising that neither the two sisters, Franziska and Camilla Meier, nor Susanne Schmaltz had joined the Frauenchor before August 1, 1859.

On Monday, August 1, Franziska wrote in her diary:

"A new life is now to begin; new horizons are opening up before me. Finally we have succeeded, after having always 'forged energetically ahead'."

The words *immer rustig vorwärts* were used by Joachim to inspire his orchestra to greater efforts. They were adopted by "The Three Crows" as their motto and signet seal.

After "the new life begins", Franziska continued writing on August 1:

"At 9 o'clock Tilla Sthamer called for me; ten minutes after 9, we were at Fräulein Glühr's on the Holzdamm. Tilla introduced me to Fräulein Glühr, then to Olga Wagner. She was supposed to introduce me to Brahms, but she neglected to do it, so I turned to Mme. Grädener (who acted as chaperone to the young girls). She was very friendly, as always. She took me to Brahms and said: 'Fräulein Meier does not know whether she is to sing first or second soprano?' Brahms looked at me in an examining manner, as though he could tell that by my face. He said, 'Could you possibly sing first alto?' The question surprised me and I did not answer immediately. Then he said quickly: 'Well, then, sing second soprano'.

"We sang Psalm 23 by Schubert and The Serenade *Zögernd leise* (Through the Darkness) by Schubert. We practiced hard; then, in the intermission, Brahms talked only to Fräulein Wiechern. I spoke to Mme. Grädener and later to Tilla, who is very unsure of herself.

"Brahms is pleased that his little flock is growing... He is very precise at practice. No one looked at him. I believe I was the only one. At first, it was hard for me to follow, then later, it came very easily.

"At 11:15 Brahms announced that if anybody wished to take the music home she should say so. I asked for one part. Brahms asked me whether it had been hard for me to follow. I answered:

'In the beginning, *very*.'

"Then he said:

'Ladies, next Monday, be here at five minutes before 9, at the latest.'

"In the meantime, my friend Susanne Schmaltz had seen Mme. Grädener and asked her if she might take part in the singing. She received a very friendly answer that she might."

"Monday, August 8 at the Wagner's. I wrote in my diary. Shortly after 8:30, Tilla Sthamer called for me to go to the Frauenchor. She scolded me terribly for not having spoken to Fräulein Wagner about Susanne Schmaltz. I remained very calm and told her that Susanne had spoken to Mme. Grädener herself and that that ought to be enough. At the door we met Mme. Grädener and Susanne Schmaltz. Susanne's heart was probably beating even faster than mine. Upstairs, I introduced her to Tilla, Fräulein Glühr, and the three Wagners. They were all very friendly. Toward 9, Grädener arrived, greeted us and was just about to start when Brahms came. We waited a little, while he amused himself. Then Avé came in and greeted me with a deep bow. Brahms and Grädener still had much to talk to each other about. Finally, at ten minutes after 9, we began: Psalm 23 by Schubert first with, then without, the accompaniment. Papa Avé was quite thrilled. Now came the main thing: two *Marienlieder--Der Jäger* (The Hunter No. 4) and *Ruf zu Maria* (Prayer to Mary No. 5)."

These were new ones, not 1 and 2 which had already been tried in June.

"Brahms said: 'The Hunter is always the first'. We practiced hard. The Hunter was difficult. At every criticism, Brahms looked straight at the two of us. We were furious. But he looked at us also at each word of praise, at every explanation, when he asked us to repeat, and when he thanked us. So then our anger turned to joy. If he would observe us, he would soon see how seriously and earnestly we take the whole thing. His remarks always amuse us. 'Fräulein Seebohm deliberately sang the wrong note!' "The altos sing too harshly!' 'Please, a little bass pedal!' Susanne and I went away together. She turned around to say goodbye to Mme. Grädener and to thank her. We went together to Kainer's, dizzy with joy. Brahms, Avé, and a lady behind us along the whole Alster St."

"Monday, August 15.   At a quarter past 6--Brahm-a-ho! Susanne could hardly withdraw from the embrace of the Heaven-born Morpheus. Finally the beloved motto *immer rüstig vorwärts*--forging energetically ahead--succeeded in arousing her."

Franziska used the word "Brahm-a-ho" more than once, obviously as an expression of enthusiasm.

Her allusion to Heaven-born Morpheus was a joke about the text of Canon No. 1 (in Op. 113). It was evidently sung by the *Frauenchor* during the first two weeks of August.

"About a quarter to 9, Susanne and I went to the Sthamer's. Tilla was far from ready. We ran through the Hohe Bleichen

and Düstern Street. We had hardly reached Pastoren Street
when Brahms appeared.

"Tilla and I sat down in the center of the 2nd sopranos. We
sang the Psalm by Schubert, two songs by Brahms, three by
Schumann, and then 'Poor Peter' by Grädener, for six-part
women's chorus--terrifically difficult! It went very badly.
I admired Brahms' patience. We practiced only the first two
parts, then in conclusion, the Psalm over again. I like
Brahms as a conductor exceedingly. He noticed us especially,
and so he should! Once when he looked at me for so long, I
tried to respond to his steady glance. Suddenly, it came
into my mind: now he is thinking of the letter! And then I
lost courage and willpower and had to look away."

Franziska's allusion to "the letter" is explained in
her diary entries of March 28 and April 1:

"I brooded over a plan I had... Jenny and Camilla have
approved and even promoted it."

The plan was to write Brahms a letter of congratulation
on his Serenade Op. 11 which had just been performed with
Joachim conducting. The Three Crows went over to the
Fuhlentwiete, the street where Brahms lived; they bribed a
little boy to deliver the letter. (See p. 79) The girls
then became nervous about their boldness.

"All day I felt as though I had committed a murder. It is
hard for me to try to fool my mother. At breakfast (a few
days later) we confessed. Thank goodness that abyss has been
crossed."

Franziska, with her facile pen, made a sketch of a little
bird carrying a letter in its beak. *Kommt ein Vogel geflogen*
(A little bird came flying, bringing me a letter), are the
words of a folksong.

(August 15 continued)
"We practiced very hard until long past 11. When Susanne
and I had already opened the door to go, we suddenly heard
the piano marvellously played upstairs. We ran up again, sat
down on two empty chairs that were standing in the doorway.
Brahms noticed us and smiled. After the playing was over,

Brahms walked ahead with Mme. Peterson. We, in high spirits, and as if in a dream, followed them."

"Monday, August 22nd, at the Glühr's. A quarter to 9... away to the Glühr's! As Brahms came in, I greeted him. He returned the greeting, somewhat surprised, but in a friendly way. We began with 'Hansel and Gretel', always, the first two parts. Finally, we were a little more successful.

"During the intermission, I spoke to Mme. Nordheim. She was complaining about the text of The Hunter -- Then I hurried back to my place. Brahms, following my example, had taken the same route. He then turned directly toward me -- 'you did not take part when we sang with the organ in church?' I answered that unfortunately this was only my fourth rehearsal. He said: 'I think we will repeat that at the earliest opportunity. Everybody enjoys singing with organ accompaniment so much.' I asked what we were to sing. Then he said: 'An *Ave Maria* that you do not know yet and a Psalm which is not ready yet.' 'Something of your own composition?' 'Yes, of mine.' 'That is fine. Shall we begin it next Monday?' He answered: 'If it is ready. I shall probably have it ready by then but the voice parts will have to be written out.' "

Each girl always copied out her own part into her own note-book (*Stimmenheft*).

"'And then we must first be through with our *ungodly* songs.' I answered: 'Oh, I like these songs very much for a change with the religious music.' 'Why certainly, Fräulein, otherwise we would not sing them at all.' 'And now the building in St. Michael's Church, which was so disturbing at the time, is finished, isn't it?' He said: 'Yes, indeed, but we are going to sing this time in St. Peter's where it will sound very much better. In St. Peter's Church, the sound is *good*. There one sings throughout the length of the church. These things are easier, too, much easier than the one by Grädener.' 'The composition by Grädener is difficult, I think, especially, for the alto.' He said: 'Yes, certainly the second alto has peculiar things to sing, notes that one is not at all accustomed to hear in succession. Quite odd intervals! difficult to strike!' I said that on the whole, I believed alto was much more difficult than second soprano. 'Altos always have to sing the notes which are missing.' Then he laughed: 'Certainly, alto is always difficult. If I let the ladies do as they pleased, not a single one would sing alto. They would all sing second soprano. That is the favorite part.'

'It is the most natural range. Most people don't have the alto notes at all. But now you have gained excellent support for the altos in Mme. Nordheim.' 'Yes', he said, 'I noticed that at once and I am very glad. She has a good voice and is musical.'

"He turned just as suddenly away and left me alone with my joy. I guess he simply wanted to know what kind of a person I am! In any case, I made the most of the moment. What will he think? He notices us. If he only keeps up this attentive observation, he will at least discover our zeal. Grädener begged for his old Peter again. After some opposition, we sang parts 1 and 2, repeating the bad places.

"Then Avé asked for Schumann's *Rosmarien, Jäger Wohlgemuth* (Happy Hunter) and *Der Wassermann* (The Merman), (all Op. 91). He thanked us. Then, after we had nearly said good-bye, Friedchen asked for one by Brahms. He let us sing both. At the crescendo in Prayer to Mary, all of us did not think of the crescendo but sang softly. I, alone, shouted on and on jubilantly. Brahms looked at me, nodded with a smile and said: 'good!' I know what that means. Such a *good* means more than when Degenhardt says: 'That you play absolutely wonderfully.'"

Degenhardt was her piano teacher.

"Monday August 29, at the Wagner's. At a quarter to 9, we went to the Sthamer's. Of course, Tilla was not ready. Then we ran to the Brahmafest. On Düstern Street, I was possessed with the idea that I must look back. I saw Brahms behind us; also, he noticed us and the distance between us became less and less. Why did that make me so nervous? We arrived at the door at almost the same time as Brahms. Fräulein Lucy Albers drove us in a cab. With her was a young lady who was called by some Fräulein Trier. Brahms opened the door to the adjoining room and let them in. Then he said to us: 'We can go straight in here; we ought to have some privileges.' I opened the door and went in. The others followed. He spoke only a few words to us about our seats and our parts, about mistakes in writing, and other difficulties. Avé was there; in my part, there were several mistakes. I showed them to him and argued with him. He asked Brahms, and the mistakes were corrected. Then Avé asked whether we would like to sing at his house, Hühnerposten 2, next Monday. He walked around among the ladies and asked every third or fourth one over and over again. To me, he said: 'You know where I live, Fräulein

- 29 -

Meier. I would like so much to have you come to me next
Monday!'

"I look forward so much to entering into this new world of
artists, to seeing lovely pictures, to talking again to Mme.
Avé in memory of these happy times. So many beautiful and
good things continually cross our path -- things with which
one never reckoned. One must only know how to enjoy them."

The evening before Brahms had written Clara Schumann
about his new Psalm (Op. 27).

"Tomorrow my girls are rehearsing a psalm which I have composed for them. I wrote it in the evening a week ago last
Sunday and it kept me happy until midnight. If you want to
look at the text, it is the 13th. As it has organ accompaniment, we shall again sing in church -- this and my *Ave
Maria* -- I have at least forty girls now."

(August 29 continued)
"The Psalm is wonderful, but Brahms had already so fatigued
himself with the bewitched Liese (Grädener's Motet) which
went very badly. It was much too hard for me, almost im-
possible to follow. I tried very hard and was ashamed of
myself before Brahms and everybody present and before myself.
He noticed it possibly and let us repeat it only twice. He
said himself that it was very difficult. Then he let us all
sing it together. I was surprised that it went as well as it
did. We listened as he talked to Fräulein Garben and we were
afraid that she was going to be forced on us as a support to
our part. But it did not come to that."

Franziska speaks of this Fraulein *Garben* who does not
appear elsewhere in the annals of the *Frauenchor*. She undoubtedly means Laura *Garbe*, one of the best singers, who
sang soprano in a solo quartette with three other members of
the chorus.

"In the wonderful Psalm, we had to join the first sopranos.
It is written for only 3 voices. It is much easier and more
beautiful, much more natural and more original than Grädener's.
God forgive me this sin!

"After our poor director had worked so hard to beat these
new things into us, he was besieged by Mme. Peterson to play
something for us! He has the reputation of being unaccom-

modating, proud, arrogant, and disagreeable. O, how can one
wrong a person like that? He played some Kreisleriana which
I did not know and which he had not played for a long time.
The poor man -- when he made a mistake, he blushed purple,
made an angry face, and shook his head. Then he asked us to
excuse his stiff fingers. They would not do what he wished
them to do. Avé then asked for the E major Sonata but Brahms
did not want to play it! 'No, that is too mighty for me, it
has gone out of my fingers entirely.' 'Then play the Symphonic Etudes!' 'O, I do not know them well. Should I not
better play the Beethoven Variations?' 'Yes, just as you
like, but do play the Symphonic Etudes.' I found him unusually accommodating. He did play us the 12 Etudes. One
could hardly believe it -- 12 Etudes!

"Before leaving, I asked if I might take Grädener's book
along. 'Grädener's book? No, you may not.' 'What a pity!'
Susanne interrupted: 'We need it so badly.' He laughed.

"I asked if we might then take his Psalm. 'My Psalm, yes,
you may take it along.' 'O, good!'

"Then we went away, Ave, Brahms, Susanne and I. Lucy Albers
went with the others, always two by two. We had to wait on
the Steinweg. Soldiers were going past. We were both em-
barrassed. Susanne, after some protest, came to our house.
We looked in the catalogue for the Kreisleriana and the
Symphonic Etudes."

"Thursday, September 1. Grund came after breakfast. I
sang Schumann, also the one with the risque words, my voice
being rusty. Then I told him about Brahms, unfortunately
showed him the music. He said, 'One should not write so high.
That is a mistake. But he is a pleasant little fellow.' I
was a bit afraid -- now everything is all right. Grund
practiced intervals with me, to get them exact. That is very
useful for me."

F. W. Grund was her singing teacher, a leader in the
musical life of Hamburg. He was conductor of the *Singakademie*,
founded in 1819, and of the Philharmonic Concerts, both important institutions. At this time, he was soon to retire.
Brahms hoped to succeed him. Grund may have been aware of
Brahms' ambition and may have resented it, showing his annoy-

ance by speaking condescendingly of the "pleasant little fellow".

"September 4. Visited Schmaltz. The old man was very humorous; he said a toll-collector got 15 Thaler an hour and Brahms only 5 Thaler. They ought to change places!"

"Monday, September 5. We went on our way to Ave's. He was friendliness personified. He shook hands with me right away and asked for the picture. I was happy."

This may have been the sketch Franziska made of Brahms. (see p. 18)

"He showed me one of Brahms and told me about Stockhausen and Von Bülow. He showed us an old *Miserere* for four women's voices by Hasse that he had found among old notes. We are to sing it next year!

"We sang the Psalm by Brahms. After practicing a long time, we had an intermission. The piano was then rolled into the middle of the room and Grädener's piece was rehearsed. 'When my grandmother had bewitched Liese, the people wanted to drown her.' Susanne and I were alone in our part. There were six on each of the other parts. Brahms noticed us and treated us differently from the others. At the end of the period, Brahms wished his own songs sung. There were two new ones, then the Angel's Greeting, when Mary Went to Church; then the Hunter and Prayer to Mary."

The two new *Marienlieder* were *Magdalena* (Easter Morn No. 6) and *Maria's Lob* (Praise of Mary No. 7).

"We decided that everybody should bring 5 *Silbergroschen* on Mondays. We hope it will amount then to about 2 *Portugaleuser*." (A gold coin of high value at that time in Hamburg.)

"Brahms played the Variations by Beethoven and the chromatic variations by Bach. Marvellous! But the piano is not as good as Friedchen Wagner's. One can hear the fingers touching the keys. I was beside myself with happiness, as if in a dream, I asked Brahms if we could take the bewitched Liese along with us. 'I don't think that would be possible.' 'Oh, the poor Liese, we need it so badly!' 'Let me ask Grädener about that. Come along with me! Grädener, may the ladies take your voice parts home with them? They would like to practice the Liese.' Mr. Grädener bowed courteously and gave us his kind permission. Brahms gave me the book. I thanked him and hurried away, elated, with Susanne through the adjoining room, pressing her hand and his as I passed them.

"Oh, how lovely this time has been. How much charm life has if one only enjoys it. And how gladly I will, as long as I am able to. In a week -- at the Wagner's. Mother went out -- I practiced Grädener's and Brahms' Psalms. Then Chopin and Brahms and how I want to practice from now on!"

"Friday, September 9.   I heard an uncanny noise outside. John brought in a card: 'A gentleman is outside and asks if he might have his music.' *Johannes Brahms!* I could hardly believe my eyes. I looked out and asked him to step inside for a moment. He entered the little room. I expressed my regrets that he had to take the trouble to come here. 'O, that does not matter at all! Avé is also outside. You have the voice parts, don't you?' I asked him to come in and speak to my parents but he looked around the corner and said: 'I have not a moment's time.' He hunted in the dark with me for the music on the piano, and then he hurried quickly away. But the goblets of bliss were spilled, the fair fruits scattered and night was darkening round about.

"In the meantime, mother had noticed who it was and came in with a light. But, too late. Camilla had heard everything from upstairs and hurried down as fast as possible. But he was too quick on his feet. I, stupid thing that I was, should have lit a light in the beginning myself! I had not the patience to embroider so I wrote in my diary instead. He thinks so well, so kindly of us here. I don't believe he is angry because of my idea and my silly letter; he will never misunderstand it! Today, a visit with a card bent over at the corner. I have kept it!"

When a caller left a visiting card bent at the corner, it meant that the call was for the whole family.

"Monday, September 12, at the Wagner's.   Susanne and I stormed in a great hurry through all the dirt. I thought for sure they would have started, but they had not. My first glance into the cloak-room assured me that no gentleman's hat was there. While we took off our coats, Brahms came. He is always so quick and also today, went in right away. When I came in, he walked up to me: 'O, Fräulein, I bothered you quite unnecessarily. The voice part I needed, you did not have.' 'Did you want your Psalm?' 'Yes indeed, I have changed something in the voice parts. I am sorry I gave you the trouble.'

"Could he only know how happy I was about this little visit and the card. Now the parts were distributed. I got a 1st soprano. I was looking for the right one when Brahms stepped up, apologized and looked with me. 'O yes, excuse me, for the other songs, quite right, for the other things, you must have your 2nd soprano.' He looked with me through all the books. Then we sang the Psalm. The high notes have been taken out. It is much more comfortable this way. How beautiful this psalm is, how pious and devout! He certainly must be a *good* person. While he was accompanying us, he looked at the picture of Schumann all time. How deeply attached he must have been to this fatherly friend.

"Then we sang an *Ave Maria*, the first in the Brahms book, written with a goose-quill. It looks so attractive. This *Ave Maria* is marvellous! Fräulein Garbe, my neighbour, was also completely overcome by our friend. During the intermission, I asked Friedchen for the money, 2 Silbergroschen. Where shall we put it? In the little drawer of the desk. Nobody really took care of this properly. I looked at the pictures. Mme. Wagner came. She had been sick, looked pale and drawn, sat down on the sofa. After I had talked there for a while to Thusnelda about Toni and her children, Avé came and asked if it were not more comfortable for us this way. Then Brahms came up to us two and said: 'Shall we begin again now?' Susanne and I went immediately to our places. We went through the *Ave Maria* thoroughly -- each part separately -- then the Psalm, then when Mary Went to Church. How simple, how peculiarly touching and impressive he has made the sound of the chimes. Absolutely wonderful!

"Then he thanked us again, as always. After a moment, Susanne asked: 'May we take the book with us?' 'Yes indeed you may!' 'We have not yet sung the Ave Maria in the chorus.' 'O, you haven't sung it yet. The others have already practiced it. Yes, with this song, you started.' We went out. I put on my coat. Susanne was just about to put on her rubbers. It was raining hard. When we heard some marvellous broken chords played, Susanne threw her rubber quickly down and we dashed in. Susanne found a chair. I was standing. Avé said it was a Sonata by Friedemann Bach. The first movement reminded me of the second page of the Tartini Sonata but then it became completely different. Ave said after he was finished: 'Typically Johann Sebastian.' I entered the music room and stood at the table. Fräulein Garbe beckoned me there. 'Here is room enough.' Brahms looked at me and smiled. He played variations of his own composition. He played marvellously -- for the last time! And now, just a word about his compositions. I told Friedchen Wagner that I was now playing his Scherzo in E♭ minor Op. 4, whereupon she said: 'All out of gratitude?' And I told her that I had played it even last spring after I had heard the Serenade. She thought that very touching. She should know how much this little man has occupied our thoughts since then. Brahma-ho! How often his name has been on our lips, how often his melodies sung. Serenade! Susanne and I, quite intoxicated, hurried through the dirty Fuhlentwiete after the Dioscuri -- Ave and Brahms -- They vanished. Who can tell me where to?"

"Thursday, September 15 at the Wagner's. Brahms was already there. We greeted each other like old friends. Quite a few were absent to-day. Brahms approached me and gave me the second part and although we sang the first, I was happy about it. Then we sang the Psalm by Brahms. 'Now it goes very well, much better!' Then *Ave Maria*. 'Be careful in the second soprano. Very good!' We were blissful! Then in the intermission, Friedchen produced the money. But he would not accept the money at all. He said, the rehearsals had given him so much pleasure that the money would spoil the whole fun for him. If only he really comes back. Friedchen is afraid that he will get a steady position somewhere. And yet, we ought to rejoice in that case. Then we sang Grädener's Wedding Motet:

'Except the Lord build the house.'

"Brahms assigned us two to a second soprano part. Then he let the third voice be sung by itself. Then he came to me and asked if I wished to join in singing the chorale. I was afraid to and I asked Susanne. She hesitated too. Brahms looked annoyed and said: 'Well, then we will first sing it through this way a couple of times.' I was very angry with myself on account of my stubborness, but it was too late. We sang it several times through and I was angry and sad that I had been so disobliging. Ave said: 'One cannot hear anything of the Chorale at all.' Brahms said sadly: 'I have just asked some of the ladies -- some of the *best* ones, to sing it, but they do not seem to feel inclined.' After a while, Brahms came up to us with three of the Chorale parts and asked: 'Who of the ladies will be so kind as to sing the Chorale?' Susanne and I were over blissful, got up as if obsessed and each one shouted I. Then he was pleased and his face looked happy. 'Now you have overcome your obstinacy.' Then I said: 'Here one only needs to count. That is easier than to hit the note.' 'Yes, if you can count, then you can sing this.' It went well. We received a lot of praise today.

"Then Brahms took leave of us: 'We shall see each other on Monday, to be sure, but I would rather say goodbye today. Thank you. On this occasion, you have helped me out in such a friendly way. Monday at 10, we meet in St. Peter's Church. If it is your wish, then we shall certainly repeat one thing or the other and then, I think, we shall begin again as soon as I return, if it gives you pleasure.'"

Here Brahms definitely proves his pleasure.

"O, this is marvellous. What wonderful anticipation! Then we went away and put our coats on slowly. I asked again if we were supposed to sit up near the organ. 'No, in the other place.' 'In the choir gallery?' 'Yes, in the choir gallery.' A strange feeling, a mixture of sadness and overwhelming joy had taken hold of me. Susanne and I got dressed while Brahms was talking to the two Völckers in the vestibule and they were trying to tell him how they had enjoyed singing under his direction. I also told him how I had always looked forward to Monday through the whole week. He bowed slightly. I was ashamed of this silly compliment. Then Brahms went in again; as we went away, he was standing at the staircase and I said: 'I thank you for all the trouble you have taken with us.' 'And I thank you.' And then we went out into the rain."

"Monday, September 19 in St. Peter's Church. At 9:30, Susanne and I were the first ones in the church. A few listeners were there too: Lucy Albers, my mother, Pastor Ritter and his wife with their nephews, Jenny and Tony Völckers, and some strangers. The man opened the gallery for us. We took off· our hats. Mme. Brandt came with her niece, the little girl from Vienna (Bertha Porubsky). Mme. Brandt has looked at a silver inkstand with a laurel wreath at the top at Brahmfeld's. It costs about 90 Silbergroschen. I think an inkstand is a very suitable present for a composer."

St. Peter's Church, Hamburg—from Gleason's Pictorial, Boston, 1854

The chorus wished to give Brahms a present, since he had refused to accept a fee for conducting.

"Time passed and the church filled up. When Armbrust and Brahms came, it was understood that Camilla was to stand upstairs. Armbrust and Brahms both spoke to her. She was happy and felt quite compensated for everything she had had to miss."

Camilla had evidently been ill and unable to join the chorus sooner.

"Brahms came down, greeted us and said: 'We shall sing here again next Monday.' Splendid! I ran down to bring Fräulein Trier up. Brahms went back up again to Armbrust. They were trying the organ. Camilla was to help. To work the bellows? O, God forbid!' Let me begin at the beginning. Susanne and I took the first places in the 2nd row. Brahms looked at us fixedly. Armbrust played too slowly and insisted that he could not see the conductor. Brahms said: 'But I can see him, so I am sure he must be able to see me, too.' We took it over again -- but this boring Armbrust could not play, it sounded terribly -- as if he were a beat behind. Brahms turned white as chalk. His lips were pale. He clenched his left fist in order to appear calm before us. I pitied him indescribably. We looked with steady gaze at the baton but we were the only ones, I believe, Poor Brahms!

"Grädener offered to beat time up there, but he could not see Brahms either. I asked: 'Can we not go up there instead? If we all stand, there will be enough room.' Brahms answered: 'We can at least try it.' So we all walked up; it was very narrow there, but we managed. Camilla crawled around between us, pulled out the stops, turned over the pages of Armbrust's music, was teased and was happy, as happy as we were. Brahms looked at us, as always. We sang the Psalm twice. The pastor's wife was called home on account of a child ill with chickenpox. Tony Weinkauf took her place. Grädener went alternately back and forth. The wonderful *Ave Maria* pleased everybody. All were beside themselves. Then came Grädener's Motet, 'Except the Lord build the house' -- Brahms asked Camilla: 'Will you play the cantus firmus?' 'If I only knew it! You mustn't scold me, if I do it badly.' 'How can I scold?'

"Susanne and I kept our excellent seats and sang the chorale; for the second time Camilla had to turn pages, she lost the

Elise, Brahms' sister, never sang in the women's chorus but she was intimate with several of the members. After Brahms had left Hamburg, she kept up her friendship with Laura Garbe and the Völckers.

count. Susanne and I counted to help her, she did not notice us, but later found the place herself. 'In the second part, you got lost once.' Then the two choir boys of Grädener's were called in. They ran like mad. The composer had to play. The smaller boy sang the chorale with us. Then I asked for the *Ave Maria*. 'Yes indeed, if you wish it, we have sung that for such a long time, we are used to it.' Then again at the end, the Psalm. Then he asked us to look again over the two new *Marienlieder*, Easter Morn and Praise of Mary, and the two Latin verses, *O bone Jesu,* and *Adoramus*. Since Brahms had given Camilla the music three times, she believed that she could very properly sing with us but she would not ask him. I plucked up courage and asked. 'O certainly, very gladly.' Then he took leave of us, met mother downstairs. She was charmed with the *Ave Maria*. Father, mother, and sister Brahms were congratulated over and over again. I would have liked to do that, but I chatted a little with Mme. Avé. I was too happy. Tony Weinkauf and I went together. She also was thrilled with the *Ave Maria*."

"Thursday, September 22 at the Wagner's. Camilla and I got ready for the 'Brahms Academy'. Camilla was in a feverish excitement. We did not want to have her between us. Tilla was not with us. The singing was, unfortunately, rather weak. The few ladies came late, they had not practiced as well as we had. We sang both the Latin Motets and both the new Marien-lieder, 'On Easter morning' and 'Praise to Mary'. He recognized Camilla immediately as the girl who had recently played the organ. He was not satisfied. I had a toothache. Then Mme. Brandt came up to me. She said the inkwell (the present for Brahms) would be ready on Saturday. Avé did not feel well. Mme. Peterson was not there at all, so there was no one on hand who could ask him to play. Brahms went into the other room, came back, went smiling through the room up to the piano. He knew what we were thinking. There was a new picture of Clara Schumann there in a thick wreath of ivy. She looks at the picture of her husband and he looks at Brahms. Then Brahms said good-bye to Camilla especially. We three went home, Avé and Brahms behind us. Camilla and Susanne turned back in to Fuhlentwiete, since Susanne had forgotten her pocketbook."

"Sunday, September 25 at the Wagner's. Got up at 6 o'clock, early Mass. Susanne came, we had breakfast, then with fever and sadness, in haste and excitement to Pastorenstrasse.

Tilla was not there. She was in church. Brahms was there, greeted us in a friendly way. We practiced hard. He was in a good mood. 'I can't stand the short rows.'"

The meaning of this is not clear. Did Brahms mean that all the chairs were not filled: The rows were short?

"'You must take breath when you can!' Ave had brought a little gray man in. Who was he? No one knew him, yet it seemed as if everybody thought everybody else knew him. Brahms asked, 'Who will take the parts by Grädener home?' No one answered. I went up to him and took them from him and found out that I was not to sing the chorale but in a chorus part.

"Then Susanne asked him: 'Couldn't we also practice this?' 'No, it would be of no use to start something else now.' Then Avé came up. He said to me: 'How I shall miss him! At least three times a week he came to see us and was always so amiable!' How true. Brahms sat down at the piano and began Bum! Bum! with the left hand. Then he rose, opened the piano and played the intermezzo from his Ballad. Then something by Schumann from the *Fantasiebilder*, the *Davidsbündler-tänze*, and from the *Kreisleriana*. I think, about eight different things. Everybody was charmed and delighted. But no one told him so. I could hardly help doing so, but then I controlled myself. We left with the books under our arms. Thusnelda said to me: 'You are certainly awfully zealous.' How could it be otherwise! We went; Avé, Brahms and the little gray man in front; eleven ladies followed. Tilla deserted us. Susanne and Camilla walked home with me but, since nobody was there, I went with them to Mme. Brandt's to take a look at the inkstand. We all liked it very much and so did Mme. Brandt and her niece.

"Brahms' song: *Die Schwälble ziehet fort* -- Op. 7 No. 4

> 'The swallows fly away, far away,
> Far to another land fly they,
> And I sit here alone and sad,' . . .

"The two Völckers, with their eternal friendliness, called us 'The Mourning Society.'

"We heard that all the publishers were besieging Brahms to surrender his treasures of music to the public. Might it be that we had some part in this?"

Franziska's suggestion here that "The Three Crows" might have influenced the publishers to notice Brahms is a reference to a "frightful plan", they had concocted in April, (1859), after Brahms Serenade, Op. 11, had been performed in Hamburg, with Joachim conducting. The girls had been more than enthusiastic about the Serenade and were convinced that Brahms was not appreciated. They thought that if they went to the music stores and asked for Brahms' compositions, they could persuade the dealers to keep his works on hand. (See p. 79) In April, she had written

"Anna and I on the hunt -- Anna went to Jowien's and so is the work finally begun. Then we went with Camilla to all the music stores and put them all on the alert -- A Brahmanen run -- Anna, Camilla, and I were again at the hunt. I, to Schuberth's, Anna to Brunner's, Camilla to Niemeyer's and then a second time to Schuberth's."

"Sunday evening, September 25. Tomorrow for the last time Brahms will be in the church. This morning, it was too wonderful, never will I forget the bliss which has moved me today. The whole week has been full of hectic excitement. Tomorrow there will be the parting from this amiable, unusual man who now is filling all our thoughts. I say with Avé: 'How we will miss him!' How we have become attached to him, how pleasant, friendly, patient, and liberal he has been toward us! I hope, when he thinks of his 'Academy', he will think especially of us, and we will think especially of him. How is it possible for me to write down the experiences of this whole week?"

"Monday, September 26, in St. Peter's Church. About 9:15, we were going to the Ritter's. Susanne and both sisters were there. We went on. In front of the closed church door, we met Mme. Brandt and her niece (Bertha Porubsky). We made someone open the door for us. Then Brahms came. 'All in black?' Some ladies had proposed that. 'We are going up, aren't we?' Camilla went after the organ blower. Brahms said to me: 'Your sister seems to be well acquainted with things here.' We were very merry. Brahms opened the door to Paradise. The ladies were weak, came late, and were not zealous. At 10:30 we were singing the Motet by Grädener, twice. Then three of the *Marienlieder*: The Angel's Greeting,

Mary Went to Church and the Hunter -- The Psalm by Schubert. It went badly. Then Brahms' Psalm and during the singing of that, he went down into the church (to listen). Grädener conducted, a little uneasily. We repeated it, the second time even worse than the first. The alto and 2nd soprano dragged behind. Then Prayer to Mary (a *Marienlieder*). Then *Adoramus* and *O bone Jesu*; and finally the *Ave Maria*. At the end of it, I asked if we could not repeat it, too. 'No, we cannot do that.' I said that down there they would think it was a second verse. Then Brahms laughed and let us sing it again.

"And now, everything is over. No, not yet. Armbrust played the New Year Greeting by Schumann and a fugue by Bach in his name. $B^{(b)}$-A-C-H (H is b natural). He could not do it! Brahms saw that I had failed during the singing of the church bells in the *Marienlied.* He frowned a little. I was terribly ashamed and Camilla put her hands over her face. Then we said goodbye to him. Mme. Nordheim was working the bellows. I went down with Susanne. We got ready. Upstairs there seemed to be crowds of people. Grädener and von Königslow asked: 'What is the matter?' The answer was: 'One of the ladies is being taught how to work the bellows.' At that point Brahms leaped out and Camilla heard the cry 'O God, it is my sister!' (see p. 79) Everybody laughed. Then I said goodbye to Brahms and wished him a good journey. He was very friendly. We went along with Mme. Peterson. She spoke enthusiastically of our friend. Avé has already invited Joachim for this winter and Stockhausen will be asked soon for February when Brahms will be here again.

"I went to Bohme's. They had only one copy of Brahms' songs in the store. They never have things because the compositions are still so new. Susanne asked at Jowien's for Op. 7 (The Swallow) in vain. He is going to get it for her.

"Tomorrow morning at 5:30, Brahms leaves. At 7:30, von Königslow, I --- 'Everybody who is a little bit of somebody!' "

VI

THE "LITTLE SINGING REPUBLIC"
1859

As soon as Brahms arrived in Detmold, where he was to conduct the castle choral society again for the fall months, he wrote to Friedchen Wagner about the inkstand:

Detmold, end of September, 1859

My dear Fräulein:

Nothing could be nicer than to be compelled to write a letter such as this one.

I think constantly of my joyful surprise when I discovered the inkstand charmingly concealed under flowers, given me in memory of the Frauenchor.

I have done so little to deserve it that I would be ashamed did I not hope to compose a lot more music for you with it; and really more beautiful tones will resound about me, when I see on my writing desk this lovely and beautiful gift.

Will you give my heartiest greetings and thanks to all those you are able to reach.

Seldom has a more pleasing joy come to me and, indeed, our gatherings will always be to me one of my favorite recollections. But not, I hope, till later years!

Your heartily sincere
Johannes Brahms [12]

He also sent a note to Bertha Porubsky, another member of the Frauenchor:

"On that last evening in Hamburg, I had great joy. I believed I knew where the inscription and the flowers came from. So, for many reasons, I wrote to Fräulein Wagner. Aye, for such a present, I may work!" [13]

And on September 30, a long letter went to Clara:

"But on Monday in the church, what a touching farewell it was! Everything was sung twice over and the audience could not help being pleased with such a concert. When I got home in the afternoon, I found a little box and, in it, charmingly hidden among flowers, a silver inkstand inscribed with the words:

'In memory of the summer of '59 from the girls' choir.'

"What will next summer not bring in the form of Psalms and songs of joy! As a matter of fact, I am becoming quite a cult in Hamburg. But I don't think that can do any harm. In any case, I am writing with even more zest and there are signs in me which suggest that in time I may produce heavenly things ---"[14]

The other section of this outpouring to his confidante Clara is particularly significant for my story, since it explains certain aspects of the *Frauenchor* that have been ignored by some biographers and misunderstood by others.

"But above all, I must tell you about my fascinating Hamburg ladies' choir. O, my dear girls, where are you? I shall certainly not stare about me when you are singing me the pretty things I have written for you; all forty of you shall stand before me and I shall see you and hear you in my mind's eye. I tell you that one of my most endearing memories is this ladies' choir, and only think of its nice, graduated arrangement, like a funnel: first the full choir, next a smaller one, for which I arranged three-part folksongs which I made them practice; and then a still smaller one, which only sang me songs for solo voices and presented me with red ribbons." [15]

The "nice, graduated arrangement of the choir, like a funnel" was, of course, pure romancing. He knew that Clara understood what he meant. The three choirs he alluded to were not sections of one large chorus but symbolized the different types of musical activity the girls engaged in with him. The "full choir" was the chorus which rehearsed all summer on

Monday mornings preparing for the church concert on September 26. "The smaller one" was Friedchen's group of intimate friends for which he set the folksongs. They had their meetings in the evening. Some, if not all, of these girls were in the "full choir". Then the "still smaller one" consisted of four girls with specially good voices who sang Brahms' solo songs and vocal quartettes. These girls were Laura Garbe, Marie Reuter, and the two Völckers. They were all in "the full choir". His reference to the "red ribbons" is some joke between him and the girls, as yet unexplained.

And then the paragraph follows:

> "I implore you to regard this as a rational letter in spite of its unpardonable sentimentalities regarding the forty girls!"

The *Frauenchor* was definitely much more to him than "an endearing memory".

Clara, apparently, had not seen the music until September of 1859. She wrote Brahms from Honnef on the Rhine about the Motets Nos. 1 and 2 of Op. 37.

> "The songs are charming and must sound quite uncommon. How beautifully the *Adoramus* flows, in spite of its classic form. I at once noticed how particularly tenderly the end fits the words *Dein köstlich Blut* before I had seen that you yourself had called attention to these words. If only I could hear all these things!" [16]

A little later, in November, she sent her approval of the *Ave Maria*, Op. 12.

> "The *Ave Maria*, with its wonderfully touching simplicity, must sound exquisite. How delightfully the voices are clothed with tender melodies and tiny ornaments. The passage in unison, *Sancta Maria*, with the F F is magnificent, and then the swell up to ora pro nobis, until the P comes again, and the close which alas! comes all too quickly. From the first bar one finds one's self in a strangely happy frame of mind and one is unwilling to be torn from it so soon. The whole

feeling reminds me of Bach's magnificent pastorale, which we
have sometimes played together."

In the same letter, came the note of criticism of the
Marienlieder which seems to have been felt by several friends:

"The songs, too (*Marienlieder*) I like extremely and among
them *Der Jäger* to begin with in which I especially like the
second part. In the second, *Ruf zur Maria*, I cannot imagine
the general effect so well, but in *Magdalena* the blending of
alto with soprano is charming. But the ones I like best are
Der englische Gruss and *Maria's Kirchgang* though I should
not care to hear them unless they were unusually well sung.
The alto parts, in particular, ought to be sung by perfect
voices if they are to be adequately interpreted."

And finally, Clara expressed her delight in Op. 27:

"And now for the Psalm! The Psalm seems to me as profound
and full of meaning as the *Ave Maria* is charming and graceful.
I put it higher as regards their musical worth although it
is easy in both works to trace the same inspired interpretation of the words. It is extraordinary how in each you
have succeeded in expressing in music the exact feeling; in
one, peace; in the other, a conflict which grows in intensity
until the final victory is won. It is so difficult to describe each separate beauty in writing, things that can be
expressed far more warmly face to face, look so cold on paper,
but I cannot stop saying this is so beautiful and that is so
beautiful; e.g. at the very beginning of the psalm I always
love that third 'Lord' in D major, and then it goes on so
wonderfully 'consider and hear me'. In 'Lighten mine eyes'
the allegro in 6/4 rises so wonderfully with the words, and
then grows softer again at 'My heart shall rejoice that Thou
helpest so gladly' -- 'so gladly' -- how beautiful that is!
And now comes one of the most beautiful passages, where the
parts continually interchange, 'I will sing unto the Lord'
up to the full chorus. Ah! if only I could hear it."

Brahms answered this letter from Detmold on November 9:

"I don't mind saying that I am very much pleased with my things.
I really believe, dear Clara, that I am growing, but you will
probably be able to understand how one 'sings unto the Lord
because he hath dealt so bountifully, so bountifully with
one'. Has he dealt so bountifully with me? --- The *Ave Maria*
and the first Psalm are also at the disposal of whoever cares

to have the parts copied out, although they will not be his property." [17]

But the tenor of his song was the ardent wish of every composer:

"I long for nothing more than to have my things performed."

Brahms had already written to Bertha Porubsky of his satisfaction that the Frauenchor was still prospering:

"I gladly learn that the Frauenchor still exists as a little republic. Shall I send songs? Gay, fresh little songs? I would like to give them directly to you, if you wish. Who has come into the alto section? I advise Fraulein G. and I would like to see others joining. And the new lady from Vienna is after all the famous pianist Marianne? Then does the *Gewisse Graue* come into the house? To whom could the ladies be better entrusted? He will not take them to the bowling alleys or compose sonatas over which one can be ruined." [18]

Who was this *Gewisse Graue* -- a certain gray old man? According to Franziska's diary for Sunday, September 25, he had once come to a rehearsal. The letter to Bertha leaves no doubt that the chorus continued to meet during the autumn of 1859. Brahms' references to "gay, fresh little songs" for the chorus was in memory of the Viennese folksongs the vivacious Austrian girl had often sung to him. She was one of Brahms' many flames and her pure soprano voice added greatly to her charm. Evidently she gave her aunt Augusta Brandt, with whom she was spending the year, some anxiety on the score of her intimacy with Brahms.

The aunt warned Bertha in Goethe's words:

"One does not crave to own the stars,
But loves their glorious light." [19]

Brahms had set the beautiful poem to music in November. 1858, so Bertha must have known it and probably had it in her own repertoire. It is Trost in Tränen, Op. 48, No. 5.

Luckily for her, she was able to accept her aunt's advice with good grace.

True to his promise, Brahms thought about music for the Hamburg girls and, in December, sent Friedchen the following letter:

Detmold, December 1859

My dear Fräulein:

Here are some new songs for your little singing republic. I hope they may assist in keeping it together.

If I can help toward this end, pray command me.

Kindest greetings to you and yours.

Most sincerely

Johannes Brahms [20]

These new songs may have been folksongs, or canons, or some of the Romances, Op. 44.

Brahms returned to Hamburg to give a concert at Grädener's Academy on December 2, 1859, performing the Schumann concerto. He conducted his own Burial Song, Op. 13, and his *Ave Maria*, Op. 12, which was sung by the *Frauenchor*. Possibly the orchestration of strings, two flutes, two oboes, two clarinets, two bassoons, and two horns was made for this performance as the wind instruments were already on hand for the Burial Song. Hübbe refers to a criticism in the *Correspondent* which said that the *Ave Maria* was "spirited, with extraordinarily delicate and tasteful treatment."

As the year drew to an end, Brahms received further encouragement about his music for women's voices. His good friend Grimm wrote:

"Have you the chorus and orchestra parts of your 13th Psalm? Will you send it to me? I have the greatest desire to study the Burial Song, *Ave Maria*, and the Psalm, and when my orchestra is assembled to go through them, if you have nothing against it, and put two pieces at least in the programme of my concert.

"If you do not say no -- then send them as soon as possible, for I should like to begin to study them next week with my girls." [21]

VII

THE AVERTIMENTO
1860

When Franziska was asked to contribute portions of her diary for the *Jahrbuch der Gesellschaft Hamburger Kunstfreunde* in 1902, she offered the entries for the summer of 1859 and regretted that she had been unable to find the diary written in 1860. This is an irreparable loss, since she must surely have had a great deal to say about the details of the *Frauenchor's* organization, the meetings, and the parties of that year. Letters and Memoirs, however, supply enough data for us to follow the chorus quite closely.

Brahms stayed in Hamburg during the winter and spring of 1860. His second Serenade, Op. 16, was rehearsed on March 28. Franziska attended and made another sketch of Brahms conducting.

One of the first letters of his 1860 correspondence went to Joachim in January:

> "I let a dozen girls sing old German songs to me. I keep them constantly at it." [22]

The "dozen girls" are also mentioned by Susanne in her Recollections:

> "At the same time there was in Hamburg a small women's chorus founded, whose leader was Johannes Brahms. I was asked to take part and this choral singing was a source of great joy for all who took part. We assembled weekly in the evenings changing to the different families' houses. Brahms composed, or set, old songs into three parts for us. There were exactly twelve of us so each voice was sung by four singers."

This, of course, refers to the small, intimate group. But the large chorus must have been "in full swing" too, according to Clara's letter of February 5, 1860.

"I am glad to hear that your Ladies' Choral Society is in full swing. What things you do write about it, to be sure!" [23]

Brahms was composing for it, probably with another concert in mind. Op. 17 consists of four numbers, unrelated to each other except that they have the same accompaniment and are all laments. The first is *Es tönt ein voller Harfenklang*, a poem by Ruperti:

I hear a harp, whose deep-voiced tones,
With love and yearning swelling ...
My love is dead ...

The idea was taken from an old elegy sung by the young lacemakers when their lovers went away.

The second song -- Come away, death -- is taken from Shakespeare's play "Twelfth Night", with the words translated into German. The third one is *Der Gärtner* (The Gardener) by Eichendorff. Both of these are men's love songs, not suitable texts for women and neither is one of his more inspired creations. But the fourth and last is an ideal song for a women's chorus. The text is a part of Ossian's Fingal, a long romantic poem about the heroes and heroines of ancient Ireland. The Maiden of Inistore mourns for her lover Trenar, slain by his enemy Cuthullin.

Brahms had thought of setting the four laments to the accompaniment of two horns and a harp. For the first and last numbers, the accompaniment is tremendously effective, transporting singers and listeners to the milieu of a remote past when hunting horns and lyres were common.

The use of the wind instruments, however, was so novel that it was the subject of much correspondence between Brahms

An invitation to an evening "sing", by the light of hurricane lamps, arranged in honor of a visit of Joachim's on March 29, 1860. Drawn by Henny Gabain, a member of the *Hamburger Frauenchor*.

and his friends.   In March, Brahms wrote to Grimm:

"On the following Tuesday, I shall try out a few things for
women's and for mixed chorus with harp and horns, to which
naturally I cannot invite people.   The harp stories or
similar things can be done again in April." [24]

Grimm praised the Fingal piece, but expressed doubt as
to the value of the others.

"Above all, I am pleased with the Fingal piece of Op. 17 and
the little Minnelied.   I wish it had a four bar ending. --
But the Fingal piece is glorious." [24]

As usual, the warmest response came from Clara:

"What made you think of a harp and horns?   I cannot imagine
what the combination of these instruments would sound like,
but it would certainly be most uncommon if not actually spell
binding.   There must have been a very pretty girl in your
choir who happened to play the harp and for whom you composed
the piece.   Provided the horns do not sound too harsh in the
hall, I should think the general effect would be full of
feeling. Please write me about it, I am deeply interested." [25]

On April 2, Brahms wrote Clara:

"Sunday evening was particularly delightful and that was due
to my girls, whom I summoned to do honour to Joachim, or
rather to do honour to them ... It was charming.   I had
spoken to Joachim about a certain girl who wore a black dress,
but when we arrived, they were all in black.   In spite of
their joy over Joachim, they insisted on putting on mourning
because our evenings were over.   Wasn't it sweet of them?
Unfortunately, we could not get a harp and two bad hornists
accompanied us.   Joachim enjoyed the whole thing very much
and I was obliged to promise to go on with it.

"It is really quite pleasant.   The girls are so nice, fresh,
and enthusiastic.   Without being soft and sentimental.   On
the way home (an hour's journey away), it unfortunately
rained, otherwise we usually have a lot of fine singing and
serenading on the road.   My girls, for instance, will walk
quite calmly into a garden and wake the people up at midnight
with their singing ... [26]

"I cannot help thinking that you must be here next time ...
The girls are always available.   I am sure you would enjoy

them immensely and you do not yet know Ossian, Shakespeare,
etc. with harp and horns."

Another composition for four women's voices, dated by
von Ehrmann April 1860, is Vineta, the poem about the sunken
city.

> Up from out the lowest depths of ocean,
> Far-off sounds of muffled evening chimes
> Tell us of the fair and wondrous city
> Deep engulfed in long-forgotten times.
>
> Deep from out my inmost heart's recesses,
> Ringing faint like far-off muffled chimes,
> Comes to me the magical remembrance
> Of forgotten love in by-gone times. (See App. D)

Vineta was published in 1868 as No. 2 of Op. 42 for a
six part mixed chorus. Why the romantic song never appeared
in the original version is unknown. That the *Frauenchor*
sang it would seem certain. It is in the *Stimmenhefte*. In
Friedchen's book, there is a date -- May 20, Sunday -- on
the pages which has her manuscript corrected in Brahms'
handwriting. This was the day of a picnic mentioned by
Clara. But more information than this -- how the chorus
liked it, whether any friends heard it, what Clara and Grimm
thought of it -- has vanished, like the sunken city itself.

Successful musical experiences led Brahms to ask his
friends to share his satisfaction. On April 15 he invited
Joachim:

> "Will you seriously consider spending some time during the
> summer in Hamburg? Frau Schumann may be here too. Then it
> would be worthwhile to continue with the *Frauenchor* in order
> to entertain you." [27]

By April 26, he had become even more determined to have
Clara in Hamburg:

> "I feel certain that you have enough youthful spirits to be
> amused by my Girls' Choir, by which I have for once indulged
> in a conventional pleasure. It is not to break up. The

choir meets on Monday evening, after which the best alto will be leaving us, so you must hear it on that evening. But you absolutely must enjoy Monday evening with us, so that you can have a taste of the most important of our distractions. It is bright moonlight just now and we will be in a particularly charming house half an hour's walk from the town. You will also be able to hear duets by me, but only on one particular day owing to the departure of the alto.

"Please be here on Saturday, because Sunday afternoon or evening I have to call upon one or two nice girls, near the town.

"P.S. You will not hear a note of my music the whole of the summer if you do not hear the perfectly charming new *Minnelieder* on Monday." [28]

He must have been alluding to the Romances of Op. 44 and the duet mentioned above was No. 3 of Op. 20, composed in April, 1860.

Before Clara came, however, Brahms wrote out some amusing by-laws for the *Hamburger Frauenchor*. He was studying Latin at the time with Dr. Hallier and so adopted an archaic style with plenty of Latin words inserted:

A V E R T I M E N T O

Whereas it is absolutely conducive to *Plaisire* that it should be set about in right orderly fashion, it is hereby announced and made known to such inquiring minds as may desire to become and to remain members of the most profitable and delightful Ladies' Choir that they must sign *in toto* (*Partoute*) the articles and heads of the following document before they can enjoy the above-mentioned title and participate in the musical recreation and diversion.

I ought in sooth (*zwaren*) to have dealt with the matter long ago, but whereas during spring's fair preamble (*preambuliret*) and until summer end (*finiret*), there should be singing, it should now be timely for this opus to see the light of day.

Pro primo be it remarked that the members of the Ladies' Choir must be present.

As who should say: They shall bind themselves (*obligiren*) to attend the meetings and practices of the society (*Societat*) regularly.

And if so be that anyone do not duly observe this article and (which God forbid!) it were to come to pass that anyone were to be so lacking in all decorum as to be entirely absent during a whole practice (*Exercitium*):

She shall be punished with a fine of 8 shillings (Hamburg currency).

Pro Secundo it is to be observed that the members of the Ladies' Choir are to be present:

As who should say: they shall be there precisely (*praecise*) at the appointed time.

But, on the other hand, whosoever shall so transgress as to make her due reverence and attendance at the society a whole quarter of an hour too late shall be fined 2 shillings (H.C.)

In consideration of her great merits in connection with the Ladies' Choir, and in consideration of her presumably highly defective and unfortunate constitution (*Complexion*), a subscription shall now be established for the never enough to be favoured (*favorirende*) and adored (*adorirende*) Demoiselle Laura Garbe, in accordance with which she need not pay the fine every time, in lieu of which a moderate (*moderirte*) account shall be presented to her (*praesentiret*) at the end of the quarter.

Pro tertio: the moneys so collected shall be given to the poor, and it is to be desired that none of them get too much.

Pro quarto it is to be observed that the manuscript music (*Musikalien*) is largely confided to the discretion of the ladies. Wherefore it shall be preserved in due love and all kindness by the honourable and virtuous ladies, married or unmarried, as being the property of others, and shall also in no wise be taken outside the society.

Pro quinto: That which cannot join in the singing is regarded as neutral (*Neutrum*); to wit: listeners will be tolerated, but be it observed, *pro ordinario*, in such wise that the due usefulness of the *exercitia* be not impaired.

The above mentioned due and detailed proclamation is herewith made public to all and sundry by the present *General Rescript* and shall be maintained in force until the Ladies' Choir shall have reached its latter end (*Endschaft*).

And you shall not only observe the above without fail, but also use your most earnest endeavours that others may in no wise or ways act or behave in a manner contrary to it.

To whom it may concern: such is our opinion and we await your judicious and much-to-be-desired approbation thereof.

In expectation whereof, in deepest devotion and veneration, the willing scribe of the Ladies' Choir, who always keeps time and is at all times theirs to command.

Johannes Kreisler, Jun.
(alias Brahms)

Given this Monday, the 30th of the month Aprilis, A.D. 1860.[29]

Brahms used the surname Kreisler instead of his own as a kind of magic password into the world of romantic poetry and music. Johannes Kreisler Jr. was a character in his favorite novel *Kater Murr* by E. T. A. Hoffman.

The facetious remark about Laura Garbe, whose beautiful voice strengthened the soprano section, was made because she was always late and Brahms never wished to begin the rehearsal without her. To her protest against the somewhat disparaging joke, Clara suggested that the allusion to her individually in the "Avertimento" would surely make her famous.

Each member received a badge. It was a three-leaved design with a circle in the center. The circle showed a B in a red ground; the three surrounding rings were marked with the letter H. F. C. *Hamburger Frauenchor*. (See p. 79 and Chapter IX)

In Susanne Schmaltz's book, she described the little insignia:

> "Each one of us had a medal with the inscription, *Hamburger Frauenchor*, which we considered sacred. In spite of that, I unfortunately lost it with the watch to which it was attached and could never find either."

One copy of the Avertimento has the following signatures:

Auguste Brandt - (aunt of Bertha Porubsky)
Bertha Porubsky - (a young girl from Vienna)
Laura Garbe - (soprano, one of the quartette)
Marie Seebohm
Emilie Lentz
Clara Schumann
Julie Hallier
Marie Hallier - (m. Prof. Junghaus and lived in Eppendorf)
Charlotte Avé Lallement - (Avé's daughter)
Friedchen Wagner - (m. Kurt Sauermann in 1865)
Thusnelda Wagner - (m. Landvogt Johannes Hübbe)
Marie Reuter - (one of the quartette)
Betty Völckers - (one of the quartette; m. O. von König-
    slow in Bonn)
Marie Völckers - (one of the quartette; m. Music
    Director Boie in Altona)

Henny Gabain - (see her sketch of Brahms)

Marie Böhme

Franziska Meier - (m. 1861 Lentz in Cuxhaven)

Camilla Meier - (sister of Franziska)

Susanne Schmaltz - (author of *Beglückte Errinnerungen*)

Antoine Mertens

Emma Grädener - (daughter of Grädener, m. Emil Hallier)

In the original of the Avertimento, the signature of Emma Grädener was missing. Instead, following the names of Antoine Mertens, probably added after April 30, were:

Emilie Burchard, Ida Begeman, Auguste Bachmann, Olga Wagner, (m. Max Rausch) [30]

Although Clara's name appears on the Avertimento, she was not present at the meeting on April 30. The signatures must have been made a few days later, after her arrival. Nor was she in Hamburg in time for the private performance of the songs with harp and horns, Op. 17, at Grädener's Academy. The last and best one -- The Fingalpiece or Lament for Trenar -- was not sung. It was not quite ready, nor were Nos. 1 and 2 of Op. 44; No. 1 being the "perfectly charming new *Minnelied*", *Der Holdseligen Sonder Wank*.

On May 6, Brahms wrote Grimm requesting him to return his *Frauenchor* compositions which Grimm was evidently inspecting:

"I am still sitting here, maybe for the whole summer. I always have the urge to go away and I can't get myself started at anything. I don't want to call my women's chorus together again. I feel that I must be on the Rhine ... Frau Schumann is coming to-morrow, for a fortnight. I would like to ask you to send my *Frauenchor* compositions. I should like to have them sung for her. Send them at once, so I can have them for Wednesday ...

"Of Ossian and the a capella *Frauenchor* things I have no voice parts. My girls have to write the voice parts themselves and it has to be done by sending them around every few days." [31]

Thus Brahms himself explained how the *Stimmenhefte* were made.

In the same letter is a significant sentence which is itself enough to prove that the activities of the large chorus and the small, intimate group were different.

> "A small group of young girls sing with me in the evenings-- German folksongs and the things I write."

Susanne Schmaltz never forgot those evenings:

> "I remember one wonderful evening in the early part of the year. We sang as usual *a capella*. We stood under a blossoming apple tree in the moonlight, Brahms conducting in the middle."

The song she quotes is the famous *Minnelied*: probably in the 3 part version. *Der Holdseligen Sonder Wank*, Op. 44, No. 1. Her recollections continued with:

> "Often, after the musical evenings with Brahms, we went home singing, dropping the members one by one."

Clara arrived on May 6 and concealed herself in a hotel until the 7th, which was Brahms' birthday. Her visit was a happy one from everybody's point of view. She recorded it in her diary:

> "I stayed in Hamburg from May 7th to 24th and spent the time very pleasantly on the whole ... We had a great deal of music together: The Serenades, The *Harfenlieder*, and to my constant joy, The *Marienlieder* and *Volkslieder* given by the Ladies Choral Society. There was one delightful evening, when Johannes told us about his childhood. On Sunday (the 20th), a party of us including some of the Ladies Choral Society, went for a delightful expedition in the steamer to Blankenese. When we got there, we sought out the most beautiful trees in the garden and sang under them, Johannes sitting on a branch to conduct." [32]

So precious was the memory of this occasion that Clara referred again to it in a letter to Brahms written on June 14, 1863.

These expeditions made such an impression on everyone who joined in them that there are several accounts. The Halliers lived in Eppendorf which, at that time, was quite in the country. Julie and Marie were in the chorus and Emil was intimate with Brahms. The chorus often met at the Hallier's and Hübbe describes an outdoor meeting there.

"A huge hothouse was scantily furnished as a dwelling. Between this and the hill was an enclosed pond situated between slopes planted with vineyards with a grotto at the south side. Above it stood a temple surrounded by trees. This garden was occasionally the scene of pleasant and cheerful meetings. In the summer of 1859, the *Frauenchor* had a picnic there. The ladies had brought paper lanterns with which the pond was encircled while the gentlemen filled the pauses in the singing with fireworks. The chorus had formed in front of the temple and Brahms often hilarious to the point of unruliness, climbed one of the trees and conducted the singing from there. Finally, the party, in the gayest mood, illuminated by the lighted lanterns, from them went a saying through the village." [33]

If the party had taken place in 1859, it certainly must have been before August 1, since Franziska makes no mention of it in her diary.

Hübbe goes on to say:

"Occasionally Brahms could be impolite even, according to conventional social ideas, especially if he noticed that they would burden him with ovations, for which he had little liking. One time he was at Avé's. As he was leaving, he was urgently reminded that a small circle of ladies awaited him in order to celebrate his birthday. He accepted with hesitation. But he returned unexpectedly. When he was asked with astonishment why he had not gone with his ladies, he calmly answered he had sent them instead of himself a fine cake."

On May 24th, Brahms accompanied Clara to the Rhine Festival at Düsseldorf. He asked the vocal quartette of girls from the *Hamburger Frauenchor* to go with them. The quartette consisted of Laura Garbe, Betty and Marie Völckers, and

Marie Reuter. Brahms showed his pride in these musical friends who sang his 3 of 4 part songs, one voice to each part. In fact, he thought so much of their talent that, later on, he begged them for a photograph. They complied with his request, inwardly rejoicing, of course, but outwardly pretending that he wanted it only to "draw up the fire in a refractory stove." [34] While they were at the Düsseldorf Festival, Brahms suggested to Clara that she give them a chance to prove their worth. She arranged an informal recital and invited a large group of distinguished people, including Joachim and Stockhausen, to hear them. Clara herself substituted for Marie Reuter who was taken ill at the last moment and could not sing. Apparently, everyone was delighted but no one now, it seems, knows which songs were performed.

Brahms stayed away from Hamburg until August 10. When he returned, he again got in touch with the singing girls and wrote Joachim on September 13:

"Here nothing happens besides my girls' singing. Before the night is over, we'll cross the Alster River for it." [35]

During the spring and summer of 1860, Brahms carried on a lively correspondence with Grimm about the *Marienlieder*. These letters are valuable as showing just why Brahms changed the *Marienlieder* and did not publish them for a women's chorus. Grimm wrote:

"My girls have sung your Psalm and the two first *Marienlieder* and gave me great pleasure thereby. If we practice on it again, it will go well. The deep altos sound very beautiful. I have a few -- It may be advisable to go cautiously with it. They won't be able to stand it, if they have to work on it much longer; the same thing for the high sopranos in the Psalm. If all goes well with the chorus at the first or second rendering -- good, allright -- to practice them is exhausting, and the result would not be satisfactory, were the personal influence of the conductor less felt than with you or I. In this sense, I think your handling of the voice parts is not practical, when all is said and done. The Psalm pleases me -- so warm, so vital and always fervent."

After Brahms had written Grimm on May 6 asking him to return his *Frauenchor* music, he received the following reply:

"Everything that I have of yours, I return herewith. Shall I write you all my ideas? --- I would not risk it for four women's voices --

"1. Because the deep voices sound much better sung by tenors and are more effective, as for instance, in your *Benedictus* -- what a wonderful piece it is!

"2. Because the studying of the piece has its exhausting difficulties. As soon as the high sopranos take breath in the pauses, they laugh at the bass struggles of the second alto voices. They are annoyed and confound them all and yearn for tones that stand within the five lines.

"This, of course, is nonsense but, for that reason, the treatment of the second alto should be cautiously handled, if the beautiful songs are to be sung with pleasure, and well. I can't help it, I myself do not care to hear the deep alto pitch through a whole song of many verses, even as the sound of a chorus, where the basses struggle exclusively below C. They must come up fresh, preferably in their middle pitch, which is really more advantageous for each voice. Besides which, the deep altos do not sound characteristic to me, as you perhaps thought (at best only in a few places). They remain (at least to me) too weak for a thorough foundation. Forgive me that this chatter has grown so long."

Then Brahms returned:

"I would like to double and thicken your thin 'buts'. I am going to try the *Marienlieder* in the next few days for 1 tenor, 1 alto, and 2 sopranos. I hope to find, in some degree, a good reception." [36]

It was clear enough what Grimm thought; he agreed with Clara's first estimate that the alto parts of the *Marienlieder* were too low and therefore ineffective.

In September, Brahms tried Joachim out:

"About the *Marienlieder*, which you probably do not know yet, I should like to bear a word -- do you like them?"[37]

- 61 -

But on October 3, of the following year, 1861, he wrote
Joachim again, this time thoroughly discouraged:

"Now I shall send my *Marienlieder* to Rieter and while, in
former times I was happy hearing them, they now seem to me
like an empty piece of paper. I don't like to send them off,
yet I could not make them any different, in short, I wish I
were rid of them!" [37]

The *Marienlieder* were published as Op. 22 in 1862 for
SSAT. In this setting however, they have not been much enjoyed. What mixed chorus will select a composition that has
no bass part? Brahms missed a chance here to further the
performance of his music. At that time, women's choruses
would have welcomed the addition of these charming and suitable
pieces to their scant literature. Brahms could readily have
made a few obvious alterations in the 2nd alto part, as Prof.
Geer has recently done in the Vassar Choral Series. Or they
can be sung exactly as they are transposed up a tone.
(Drinker Choral Library U. of P. Choral Series No. 75) (See
p. 22) The only one of the seven that cannot be sung by
merely transposing it is No. 3, Mary's Journey, which was not
in the *Frauenchor's* repertoire and must have been composed
in the new arrangement. And the songs, in their original
form, had evidently pleased enough people to justify their
continued existence. Franziska never mentioned any difficulty
on the part of the chorus with them; Clara noted in her diary
that she heard them to her "constant joy". Even some years
later, Franz Wüllner performed them at the Cologne Conservatory, when Teresa Behr Schnabel was a pupil there. She sang
the 2nd alto part in the chorus and remembers the *Marienlieder*
with satisfaction.

VIII

PUBLIC PERFORMANCE
1861

Between 1859 and 1863, Brahms composed the twelve Romances for four part women's chorus, published in 1866 as Op. 44. They are all in the *Stimmenhefte*. No. 1, *Der Holdseligen Sonder Wank*, is written in two versions, in three parts and in four. Obviously, the three-part song was intended for the group of twelve girls, four to each part, as Susanne Schmaltz explained. In one of Friedchen Wagner's books, the same enchanting melody is set to words adapted for a bridesmaids' song. But for what couple the felicitation was intended, we have not the slightest clue.

1. *Der Holdseligen Sonder Wank*; poem by J. H. Voss,
   To my darling one, strong and gay,
   Love is bidding me sing to-day ...

2. *Der Bräutigam*; poem by J. von Eichendorff,
   From every mountain sounding ...
   I hear the voice of spring.

3. *O, Fischer auf den Fluten, Fidelin*; Italian popular
   song.
   O, fisher come thee hither, Fidelin.

4. *Wozu ist mein langes Haar*; Slavic folksong.
   O, why have I long and curly hair?

5. *Die Mühle*; poem by von Chamisso.
   The sails of the wind mill are sweeping.

6. *Die Nonne*; poem by L. Uhland.
   Within the cloister meadow
   A weeping maiden sighs.

7. *Nun stehen die Rosen*; poem by P. Heyse, *Aus dem Jungbrunnen*.
   The red, red roses are blooming
   And Love again his snare has set.

8. *Die Berge; Aus dem Jungbrunnen*.
   The mountains are cold, and the mountains are steep.

9. *Am Wildbach; Aus dem Jungbrunnen*.
   The willows by the water
   are waving night and day;
   our love will never waver,
   nor will it pass away.

10. *Und gehst du über den Kirchhof; Aus dem Jungbrunnen*.
    And when you go to the churchyard,
    A newly made grave is there ...

11. *Die Braut*; poem by W. Müller.
    This gay colored apron, thou, my mother gave me,
    It were waste to buy it, waste to weave and dye it.
    By to-morrow morning will my tears have made it
    Look no longer blue but colorless and faded.
    (See p. 92)

12. *Märznacht*; poem by L. Uhland
    Hark! The March wind is roaring,
    The torrents are gushing to-night, hark!
    Shyly filled with delight
    Loveliest Springtime is near.

Every one of these poems expresses the spirit of romantic love and the longing to live life to the full in the green forests, near the rippling streams, where flowers bloom and birds sing. "The Bridegroom" (No. 2) is the very essence of romance, and combines the expression of a subjective emotion with the objective quality of a ballad in a way that makes the text ideal for a chorus.

From every mountain sounding
Rejoicing echoes ring,
O'er hill and dale resounding
I hear the voice of spring.
Thru castle yard is ringing
A summons clear and gay,
My love to me is singing,
'Come ride with me away.
'Ah, whither are we going,
So fast o'er dale and hill?'
The breeze is softly blowing
The sleeping wood is still.
Away! together fare we,
The moonlit forest thru.
The night is still; what care we?
Where Love may take us two!

The music, too, rushes on like the steed that carried the lovers. It is one of Brahms' most successful and appealing pieces for women's chorus.

Another four part composition from the same period, and also written in the *Stimmenhefte*, is *Es geht ein Wehen* by Paul Heyse, *Aus dem Jungbrunnen*. For some unknown reason, it was not included in Op. 44, and was never published for women's voices, but is now available at Drinker Choral Library U. of P. Ch. Ser. 22. It appears for mixed voices in

Op. 62, No. 6 slightly changed at the end.   The beautiful
words recommend it for any setting:

A sigh goes floating thro' the wood,
  I hear the wind's bride singing.
She's singing of her Dearest one,
  and 'til she is his very own,
With anxious heart she must go on,
  across the wide world winging.
The song that thus so ghastly sounds,
  the sound so wild, so troubled,
Has set my heart on fire, my precious one!
A thousand, thousand times, good-night!
The day will come, before we know,
  when we will be together.

And the music is especially effective when sung by women.
The first verse, about the wind's bride, sounds more ethereal
and mysterious than is possible when men's voices participate.
The almost magical contrast which comes when the voices move
up half a tone to the affirmation of human love is therefore
all the greater.   But no mention is made of this treasure
for women's voices by the singers or other friends!

Clara came to Hamburg on January 9 and stayed at the
Halliers.   The happy memories of the previous year induced
her to invite the *Frauenchor* to sing at her concert on
Tuesday, January 15, at 7 P.M. in the great Wörmer's Hall.
The programme for this great occasion read as follows:

CONCERT

by Clara Schumann

with the kind cooperation of a Ladies' Chorus

and

Messrs. Joseph Joachim, Johannes Brahms, Nicolaus
Schaller (harp)

Programme

1. Sonata for piano and violin .... Beethoven Op. 47
     Clara Schumann and Joseph Joachim

2. Songs with harp and two horns .... J. Brahms
     a. *Es tönt ein voller Harfenklang*   (Fr. Ruperti)
     b. *Komm herbei, Tod*   (Wm. Shakespeare)
     c. *Der Gärtner*   (J. von Eichendorff)
     The Hamburger Frauenchor

3. Symphonic Etudes .... R. Schumann Op. 13
     Clara Schumann

4. Andante and Variations for Two Pianos ...... R. Schumann
     Clara Schumann and Johannes Brahms

5. Barcarolle and Scherzo for violin .... Spohr
     Joseph Joachim

6. Songs for Women's Chorus .... J. Brahms
     a. *Minnelied*   (J. Voss)
     b. *Der Bräutigam*   (J. von Eichendorff)
     c. *Gesang aus Fingal* (Ossian) with harp and horns
     The Hamburger Frauenchor

7. Nocturne .... Fr. Chopin
     Gavotte .... J. S. Bach
     Clara Schumann

The concert was repeated in Altona on January 16. Clara's own account of her visit is in her diary:

> "Johannes made my stay very pleasant by his kindness and his often beautiful playing. He played a great deal of Schubert."

> "Tuesday, January 15.   I gave a soirée. Joachim came on purpose to play and Johannes also played some pieces for two pianos with me. Besides these, the Ladies Choral Society sang some of his Ossian songs with harp and horn obligato. They are pearls. How can one help loving such a man?"

> "January 16.   Soirée at Altona. Johannes' songs again and also Joachim, magnificent. I can well put up with concerts of this kind. *Then* it is a joy to have music." [38]

In 1861, the public appearance of a Ladies' Choral Society was quite unusual. If a performance were given by a women's chorus, it took place in a private house before invited guests and had the nature of an entertainment. Or else, a concert was given as part of the activities of the music school, in the Conservatory building. A third and not so general an outlet for a women's chorus was in a Protestant Church, upon the occasion of a wedding, a funeral, or a christening. But it was not until the 20th century that a women's chorus appeared in public on the concert stage on a par with a mixed chorus, an orchestra, or a soloist. In Germany, the change in custom did not take place until 1912, when Margarete Dessoff conducted her Frankfurt women's chorus at the Brahms Festival.

Clara's concert of January 15, 1861, therefore, was very important in the annals of women's choruses. It had immediate repercussions because, through it, people became familiar with the *Harfenlieder*. On April 5, Frau Franziska Cornet, a singing teacher in Hamburg gave the Fingal piece at a concert of her 40 pupils. And on April 27 of the following year, Clara wrote Joachim from Paris:

> "The German Choral Society is going to get the *Harfenlieder* (Op. 17). I have been happy about this for days past." [39]

The Völckers' house in Hamburg, where nightingales sang and where the Frauenchor often met.

There is every indication that the *Frauenchor* was active during the winter of 1860-61. Brahms was in Hamburg and the amateurs of the city had evening after evening of pleasure with music. Franziska told Frau Marie Zacharias, who organized the material for the *Jahrbuch* of 1902, that she remembered March 3 vividly since she became engaged on that evening. The *Frauenchor* met and practiced the canon *Märznacht* (Op. 44, No. 12) with special diligence.

During the summer of 1861, Brahms lived at Frau Dr. Rösing's in Hamm. She was the aunt of Marie and Betty Völckers and lived next door to them in a low, broad country house at the corner of the Schwarzenstrasse. Here, Brahms had a studio to himself where he could work undisturbed but have pleasant company when he desired it. He thoroughly enjoyed the informal gatherings at these two houses, as well as at the Wagner's, at the Brandt's, and at the Hallier's who always welcomed artists, poets, and musicians.

At the end of October, Clara returned to Hamburg and gave another concert on November 16, 1861, at which she played a piano quartette by Brahms from manuscript (Op. 25). Again, she invited the *Frauenchor* to participate. This time, sixteen ladies sang six songs which were received by the audience "with vigorous acknowledgement." But which ladies and what songs?

During most of the spring and summer of 1862, Brahms continued to live at Frau Dr. Rösing's, whose place he had grown to love. The Völckers were still next door and the informal music went on. After several years, when he had left Hamburg and Marie Völckers, as Frau Professor Boie, had gone to Bonn to live, he wrote her:

"If you have any more photographs taken, bear in mind the two houses, which are very dear to both of us and then think

Brahms' dedication in one of Betty Völckers' Stimmenhefte:
"I bless the house . . ." (from the *Brautgesang*).

of me again, too. There is no other time that I would rather recollect! I can think of nothing better." [40]

In one of Betty's books, he wrote a dedication:

"As a friendly remembrance of our sociable music making."

Curiously enough, he used the phrase from the *Brautgesang* to honor her house:

"I bless the house ..... "

Marie Völckers Boie shared Brahms' feelings:

"Often distinguished guests asked if they might visit us. Frau Schumann, Joachim, and others. And although we lived so far from the city, Brahms always wanted the *Frauenchor* to meet at our house. What a source of pure joy and beautiful memories that time affords! It was so wonderful that I cannot describe it or recreate it in words. Brahms came over almost every day, played for us far into the night, fulfilling every wish and every request willingly. I also had the good fortune to be his pupil. With Fräuleins Garbe and Reuter, we sang the beloved songs; he gave the note and beat time a little and we (called by him "his girls' quartette") competed jubilantly with the nightingales of the garden. He sent us over new songs ..." [41]

Everybody mentions the nightingales in the gardens and the beauty of their song. Certainly, it must have been these birds that inspired him to set *Die Verzauberte Nachtigall* (The Enchanted Nightingale), write it out for them in his own hand, and take it to the girls who "competed jubilantly with the nightingales."

To resume Marie's story:

"He sent us over new songs ... one was the splendid *Und gehst du über den Kirchhof* (And when you go to the Churchyard), Op. 44, No. 10. Another one we practiced was *So hab' ich doch die ganze Woche* (Through all the week I had awaited), published as Op. 47, No. 3 for solo voice. At our request he set for us *Wenn ich ein Vöglein wäre* (If I a bird could be) from Schumann's Genoveva; *Mein Schatz ist nicht da*, (Far over the sea is my own dear lad) published as Op. 14, No. 8; *Morgen muss ich fort* (To-morrow I must go); and still other songs in four parts."

In one of Marie Völckers' Stimmenhefte, there are several insertions in **Brahms'** handwriting.   One of these is *Die Verzauberte Nachtigall* (The Enchanted Nightingale).

Notation from Marie Völckers' singing-book.

Brahms' 3 part version of *Mein Schatz ist nicht da,* (op. 14, no. 8) as composed
for Betty and Marie Völckers and Laura Garbe in April 1862. In the last
bar of the first system and in the sixth bar of the second system,
the signs √ indicate repeat for those bars. Brahms has
substituted the numbers 1, 2, 3, 4, 5 to save himself
the work of copying.

Attached to one of Marie's *Stimmenhefte* is a card inscribed in the thinnest and finest German script:

"If I a bird could be;" and "Far over the sea is my own
dear lad." Manuscript by J. Brahms for Fräulein Garbe,
Betty and me. Written on Easter eve April 8, 1862."

The three part arrangement of *Mein Schatz ist nicht da*
is particularly interesting since this was one of the songs
composed while Brahms was under the spell of Agathe at
Göttingen in 1858. (See Chapter III) The words have the
added value of being appropriate for girls.

> Far over the sea,
> Is my own dear lad,
> And I think of him oft,
> And my heart is so sad.
> Fair blue is the sea,
> And my heart full of pain,
> There is no joy for me
> Till my love comes again!

The solo version must have been the earlier for the first
love and the trio was the result of his infatuation for
Laura Garbe's equally beautiful soprano voice. Only this
time, Betty and Marie Völckers claimed attention too. That
the three part version became appropriated by the *Hamburger
Frauenchor* can be seen from the neat edition in Franziska
Meier's book, *Versammlung No. 3*.

When the autumn came, the good times were over and, unfortunately, forever. Brahms went to Vienna. Although he
had fully intended to return and did return the following
summer, he never called his *Frauenchor* together again. It
was not because some of the girls had married and moved away--
they could have been replaced by others. It was not because
he had lost interest in the women's voices. His contacts
with different groups of women in Vienna dispose of that

"Mein Schatz ist nicht da". This version is from Franziska Meier's book, Versammlung No. 3.

suspicion. The real reason was that his attitude toward his Hamburg friends had changed. He was deeply hurt that they had not offered him the leadership of the *Singakademie* and the Philharmonic Orchestra when the opportunity to engage new directors arose. The citizens of his native town failed him at a critical moment of his career. While the members of the *Frauenchor* were not themselves influential enough to have sponsored him, their families could probably have exerted pressure upon the managers of the Hamburg musical institutions. As it was, he felt too angry to continue his formal association with the Ladies' Choral Society.

The girls were still singing, singing the music he had given them. One day, a few of them had gone to Baurschen Park in Blankenese for a picnic and were surprised to see Brahms walking alone, deep in thought. They wondered how to attract his attention until they agreed: "We will simply sing one of our old songs!" So they chose the folksong "There stands a tree in Odenwood." At the sound of the familiar voices, Brahms forgot his ill-humour and joined the singers.

Canon No. 12 in Op. 113 is dated Hamburg, May 7, 1863 and may have been a birthday present from Brahms to his old friends. He celebrated his 30th birthday in Hamburg, we know, and probably several members of the *Frauenchor* were there, singing this new canon and the others he had previously written for them.

1. *Göttlicher Morpheus*; text by Goethe.
   Heaven born Morpheus.

2. *Grausam erweiset*; text by Goethe.
   Cruel, ah cruel, has love been to me.

8. *Ein Gems auf dem Stein*; text by Eichendorff.
   A ram on the height.

10. *Leise Töne der Brust*; text by Rückert.
     Softly plucking the chords.

11. *Ich weiss nicht*; text by Rückert.
     I wonder why the dove so sad is cooing.

12. *Wenn Kummer hätte zu tödten*; text by Rückert.
     If grief were able to kill me. (dated May 7, 1863)

I have numbered these as they appear in Op. 113, published several years later. There are three other canons, however, written in the *Stimmenhefte* that were not included in Op. 113. One of these is:

Töne, lindernder Klang.
    Music however soft, thou hast no cure for my anguish.

It was later published for S. A. T. B. but not in the original key of G minor. The musical feature of it is the continuing change of key back to the original scale. At the entry of each voice, a sharp is added to the preceding key. With four voices each entering 3 times, the cycle is completed. (See Appendix D)

The other two appear in Brahms' handwriting: *Mein lieb, blau Blümelein* and *Der Herr erbarm sich unser*. They are the refrains to a song which begins *Dem Himmel will ich klagen* and to the *Lied der geissel brüder*. (See p. 111)

The history of the *Hamburger Frauenchor* ends on Brahms' birthday, May 7, 1863. It is still an incompleted history with many discrepancies in the biographers' accounts and many puzzling questions still unanswered. For example, was the chorus supported by the piano at the rehearsals? If so, who was the accompanist? No mention is made of one. In the informal gatherings, did Brahms improvise accompaniments to the folksongs? How much we should like to know about such details!

But, in substance, the diaries, letters, and other written accounts agree. One of the Völckers' *Stimmenhefte* contains a letter from Bertha Porubsky in which she has inscribed the first bars of the song; "Oh God, how sad is parting," followed by an expression of her own feelings when she left Hamburg:

> "How hard has been my parting from a circle in which I found so much love ------ "

And, in Marie Völckers' own words, the years 1859 to 1863 evoked "beautiful memories" and the *Frauenchor* was "a source of pure joy" to the members and to Brahms.

As a conclusion to the records of the *Hamburger Frauenchor*, Friedchen Wagner's Memoirs serve very well. One passage shows the warm friendship that existed between her and Brahms:

> "During one of the last lessons before he left for Vienna, I asked him to write something for me as a souvenir and he promised me to do so. Since I preferably played things by Bach under him, he chose a chorale melody, elaborated by him (also for the organ). *O Traurigkeit, O Herzeleid.* He did not give it to me during the lesson, however, but promised that I should soon have it. It was very hard for me to say goodbye to him; I had so very much to thank him for. As I was very sad, I did not open the piano for some days, but when I did open it again, I found there the beautiful gift I had been promised: the marvellous chorale prelude to *O Traurigkeit, O Herzeleid.* My maid told me that Herr Brahms had put it in the piano himself."

Another recalls the beginnings of the *Hamburger Frauenchor* and some of her most vivid memories:

> "While I was taking lessons from Brahms I asked him one morning -- since my two sisters and I often sang together -- to compose folksongs for that purpose, which he was very willing to do. After a short time, several young ladies came to take part in the singing, and thus gradually a women's chorus was formed in my parent's house. Rehearsals took place every Monday morning at 10 o'clock and Brahms composed

a number of folksongs for us. The chorus grew to twenty members and gave great pleasure to Brahms and us.

"The very numerous statutes which Brahms worked out are still in existence. We members received a neat insignia which was made of pure silver, particularly beautifully made. The letters B. F. C. were on three circles.

"My sister Thusnelda and I, Laura Garbe and Marie Reuter were always present. We sang several times in church, the last time in St. Peter's, under his leadership. Often also outside the city in Hamm, at the Völckers' in the Schwarzenstrasse. Marie Völckers was also a pupil of Brahms. At the end of the Völckers' garden, somewhat elevated, stood an arbor in which some of the members of the chorus sang together with me and my sister Thusnelda Hübbe. In the evenings, after the rehearsals, Brahms always played for us and then accompanied us home. One evening, several members of the chorus had assembled in the garden and, since we were all in a very happy mood, we went to an inn and sang there more songs."

Friedchen's statements of fact do not agree word for word with other accounts but memories, after all, are not daily recordings. To one who has reached middle age, the events of the past merge into one another. One cannot remember whether one had a pleasant evening this summer or that. Her impressions, however, correspond to everyone else's who shared those happy experiences.

Title page of Camilla's new song-book (see p. 78)

IX

THE WOMENS' CHORUS
IN CUXHAVEN AND VIENNA
AFTER 1863

When Franziska Meier married and went to live in Cuxhaven, she was determined to organize a women's chorus there. Her first problem was to get copies of the music sung by the *Hamburger Frauenchor*. Her reminiscences in the *Jahrbuch* of 1902 explain her first step in overcoming this difficulty:

"My sister Camilla asked Brahms whether he had any objection to our singing the folksongs and choral songs by him in our little chorus in Cuxhaven. She received the following most gracious letter."

Dear Fräulein:

Permit me to write you somewhat hastily and briefly that I do not begrudge you any of the things you wish, which you yourself can get together.

I myself do not possess a single note and do not know who may have saved anything.

Unfortunately, my unsettled life prevents me from guarding the memory of lovely musical and sociable pleasures.

The following pieces have been published: the *Harfenlieder*, *Ave Maria*, and in the near future will appear some sacred songs, *Adoramus*, *O Bone Jesu*, and *Salve Regina*.

Give my regards to all of you ...

J. Brahms

In 1865, Franziska could not genuinely have regarded this as a "gracious letter". Nor did others who read it. Some of Brahms' biographers have used it as proof that he attached no value to the women's chorus in Hamburg or to the music he composed for it. Seen in the light of his disappointment in Hamburg, however, the indifferent tone of the letter is clearly explained. It was certainly far from the truth that he did not "possess a single note" of the music he had written for women's voices. At that very time, he was negotiating with different houses for its publication. Obviously, he was still too angry with his Hamburg contemporaries to help even his loyal friends.

With characteristic energy, Franziska and Camilla made new copies of the *Stimmenhefte*, writing out the complete parts of the songs. Both music and words in these books is clear and legible, in contrast to the writing in the old *Stimmenhefte*, which is extremely difficult to decipher.

According to Anna Lentz, the thinner script with the open half-notes was the work of Camilla. The volume marked Franziska Lentz, *Versammlung No. 3*, contains a verse by Camilla:

> *In treuer Liebe abcopiert*
> *Und meinem Fränzchen dedicirt,*
> *Wenn mir ein Fehler drin passirt*
> *Irn Schwesterliebe subtrahirt*

> Copied out in the spirit of true love
> And dedicated to my little Franziska,
> If there should be a mistake,
> Sister love will subtract it!

In the books written by Franziska, there are charming examples of her "sister love": drawings to illustrate their favorite songs. Franziska's daughter, Anna Lentz, gave the interpretation and wrote the captions for us on the page opposite the sketch.

1. Beginning in the upper left hand corner of the page, the girl and boy sitting near the spider-web illustrate one of the Romances of Op. 44, No. 7.

> *Nun stehen die Rosen in Blüte*
> *Da wirft die Lieb ein netzlein aus.*

> The red, red roses are blooming
> And Love again his snare has set.

2. The little man, with knapsack and outstretched hand, depicts *Ich fahr dahin*, an old folksong in which the young man, as he goes away from home, trusts his heart to his dearest wife, begging her to remain in her cottage and be true to him.

> "The day has come, when thou and I,
> My dearest one must say good-bye,
> I leave my heart behind with thee,
> So far away; but it must be!
> Far, far away; far, far away."

3. At the bottom of the page, on the left hand side, a boy stands looking at a tall tree which, in the sketch, winds from the bottom to the top of the page. He is thinking of the times he went to the forest of Oden with his loved one and listened to the birds sing.

> *Es steht ein Baum in Odenwald*

> There stands a tree in Oden wood

4. Then turning to the bottom of the right hand side, a singer stands with his guitar. On account of the carnations, Anna Lentz thought that Schumann's 3 part song, Op. 29, No. 2, was intended.

> *In meinem Garten die Nelken .....*

> The pinks that bloomed in my garden,
> Are turning pale and wan,
> Roses have faded and withered,
> Since you are gone.

5. Above, a rather belligerent looking girl laments that the thistles and thorns sting no more than the false tongues gossipping about her. The folksong is *Mein Schatz ist auf die Wanderschaft*.

My lover is away, wandering.

6. Next, a maiden is weeping about her sad heart.
Mein Herzlein thut mir gar zu weh!

My heart is so sad.

And last, at the top right hand corner, Franziska has drawn two lovers galloping away on horseback. This is *Der Bräutigam* (The Bridegroom), Op. 44, No. 2.

My love to me is singing,
'Come ride with me away'!

The other page of drawings illustrates some of the girls' activities in connection with Brahms and the *Frauenchor*. They have already been explained on pp. 24, 27, 40, 41 and 56.

In Cuxhaven, Franziska not only organized the chorus but conducted it herself. Anna's letter of July, 1935, to me, written in her own English, gave some interesting details:

"The choir of my mother in Cuxhaven was not so very important and, as far as I know my mother let never sing in public, because the members had little practice, and sang only for enthusiasm. It kept up a good deal of years interrupted by the childbeds of my mother. She had ten children, but the difficulties were great because the members were not at all accustomed to read notes, had domestic duties, and in the storm, Cuxhaven with bad roads, in the old times they had much trouble to assist the practices. In the beginning, my mother had to write all the *Stimmenhefte* herself, until gradually the ladies learned to write them. The first exercises were when I was a baby, 68 years ago, and I have often been disturbing the singing by crying aloud. Later, my mother had founded a second choir in the 80's in which I and three sisters joined."

In the meantime, Brahms himself had been carrying on with another women's chorus. When he went to Vienna in 1862, he found some of his Hamburg friends already there. Karl Grädener was organist at the Evangelical Church and also professor at the Conservatory of the *Gesellschaft der Musikfreunde*. Through Grädener, Brahms met the von Asten family. Frau Schuttenmayer von Asten lived in Gundelhof with her three daughters, Marie, Julie, and Anna. When Clara Schumann was in Vienna, she always stayed with them and gave Julie piano lessons. Brahms now took over the young lady as pupil and went to the von Astens several times a week. One day, he happened to say that he missed the *Hamburger Frauenchor*. Whereupon, Julie and Anna (who later became a singing teacher at the Berlin *Hochschule*) invited several ladies from the *Singverein* to their house and so organized a small women's chorus to be conducted by Brahms. These women were good musicians and all had wonderful voices. Several of them sang in concerts. Karoline Bettelheim, Ottilie Hauer, Marie Geisler, and Frau Anna Franz, née Wittgenstein, belonged to the group and became life-long friends of Brahms. Through them, he was introduced to many people of influence in the musical world.

In April, 1863, the von Asten chorus gave a concert for invited guests at which they sang six of Brahms compositions for women's voices.

In December, he composed a *Salve Regina* for the chorus, in which he challenged the skill of these expert singers. The solo voices have an extremely difficult canon to sing while the chorus breaks in with its *Halleluia*. The *Salve Regina* was published in 1866 with *Adoramus* and *O Bone Jesu* (of Hamburg days) as Op. 37 and immediately attracted the attention of critics. A Catholic paper commented upon the "spiritual, serious, and artistically wonderful" quality of the music: high praise for a Protestant composer who might easily have offended those with scruples about an unorthodox use of liturgic texts.

Julie, Anna, Marie von Asten and their friends kept up their chamber music for a year or more. Anna took lessons from the well-known singer Pauline Viardot-Garcia. One summer, Anna and her other pupils asked Brahms to write them a serenade that they might celebrate their teacher's birthday. This he did and conducted the performance by the young ladies outside Mme. Viardot's house early in the morning. Friedländer says that the three part folksong *Da unten im Tale* (Down in the Valley) was placed at the disposal of Julie and Anna for this occasion but unfortunately he gives no hint as to the musical setting of the folksong in a Serenade. [42]

While in Vienna, Brahms renewed his friendship with Bertha Porubsky, who had married Artur Faber. When their second child was born, Brahms sent her his famous lullaby *Guten Abend, Gute Nacht*, reminiscent of the lovely folksongs she used to sing in Hamburg when she was visiting her aunt Augusta Brandt and singing in the *Frauenchor*. The melody of one of her favorite waltzes was incorporated into the piano accompaniment.

Later, Bertha organized a chorus which met in her house. It was both a mixed and a women's chorus, conducted by Eusebius Mandyczewski. Many of Brahms' compositions were sung by the "Faber-Chor".

In Vienna, the aristocrats were real lovers of music. Some women belonged to several choruses and went from house to house, singing for many hours a week. Mandyczewski was popular as a conductor of these groups and devoted years of his life to collecting, editing, and also composing music for women to sing. In 1892, he married Albine von Vest, a singing teacher and also a conductor of a women's chorus of her own. After their marriage, Mandyczewski fell heir to Albine's chorus and, together, they kept it up for many years. Much of their knowledge about choral literature for women was passed on to Margarete Dessoff, who then brought it to New York where she came after the First World War and founded the Adesdi Choir.

Mandyczewski shared Brahms' interest in canons. The two friends carried on a voluminous correspondence as to the best way of scoring them. In one letter to Brahms, Mandyczewski made a joke on the text of "Heaven-born Morpheus" -- the God of Sleep. He changed the name to "Orpheus" -- God of Singers. "Heaven-born Orpheus, where are the parts to the Canons? I need them next Monday, since we wanted to sing them in Purkersdorf, and without canons, it is no fun. I know well that you do not approve of it, but I would like to ask, if I might softly come into the apartment and look there for the Canons." [43] He wanted the Canons for the singing society he conducted in Frau von Hornbostel's house at Purkersdorf. She was the former Helène Magnus, a pupil of Stockhausen and an excellent interpreter of Brahms' songs. Brahms often went to the von Hornbostels and sometimes attended the rehearsals of the women's chorus. The first time he came, he was surprised to hear the text of the folk-song about an imaginary little man, who brought candy to good children and switches to bad ones, transformed as follows:

Villa, villa, vill, Herr Brahms is coming,
Villa, villa, vill, what does he bring?
Villa, villa, vill, such lovely canons
Villa, villa, vill, for us, tonight, to sing. [44]

Frau von Hornbostel and Mandyczewski had developed the chorus to a pitch approaching perfection. They agreed with

Brahms that "Canon singing is, above all, a social entertainment and must be able to be improvised. They are not
adapted for large choruses ..." [45]

It was probably the virtuosity of this group that led
to the selection of thirteen canons for Op. 113. In a letter
to the publisher, Brahms wrote:

"Op. 113 is an opus for which I have special fondness and
special wishes. First, I wish to call attention to the fact
that these are not difficult canons -- but that they are
amorous, innocent little verses which ought to be easily and
gladly sung by beautiful girls. I think that private
quartette singing has come into fashion partly through my
efforts in that line and I wish that the same may become
true with regard to the singing of canons." [46]

Brahms certainly succeeded in making the canons attractive
for small groups. Nos. 3 and 4 of Op. 113 are familiar folksongs ---- "What bird is that in the pine-tree there" and
"Sleep baby sleep." They are simply enough arranged for
children to sing. One never tires of the others, composed
with such technical skill including the use of double canons,
inversions, and canons in contrary motion. No. 13 of Op. 113
is especially interesting -- "Love ever sings the same sad
song." The form of it is like that of the old 13th century
round, "Sumer is a 'cumen in." Four sopranos sing a canon
and two altos imitate each other as a foundation for the
composition making a double canon. As an added charm, the
melody is *Der Leiermann* by Schubert. And indeed, all the
canons have lovely melodies. Brahms never sacrificed beauty
of tone to form but gave each one a lyric impulse that makes
them delightful to sing. Best of all is March Night, No. 12
of Op. 44.

> Hark! the March wind is roaring,
> The torrents are gushing to-night, hark!
> Shyly filled with delight
> Loveliest Spring-time is near!

It is in strict canon form throughout but the whole mood of the song changes with the last two lines. It becomes a romance of unexpected brilliance; for that reason, probably, it became one of the *Lieder und Romanzen*, Op. 44.

March Night had been in the repertoire of the *Hamburger Frauenchor* with the canons Nos. 1, 2, 8, 10, 11, 12 of Op. 113. On the page upon which No. 12 is written in Marie Völckers' *Stimmenheft* is the date 1868. Marie and her friends evidently did enjoy "private quartette singing" long after Hamburg days.

In Op. 113, Nos. 3, 4, 5, 6, 7, 9, 13 belong to the Vienese period:

3. *Sitzt a schöns Vögerl*; folksong text and melody a 4.
   What bird is that in the pine-tree there?

4. *Schlaf, kindlein, schlaf*; folksong text and melody a 3.
   Sleep, baby, sleep.

5. *Wille, wille, will*; folksong text and melody a 4
   The man is coming.

6. *So lange Schönheit*; text by Hoffman von Fallersleben a 4.
   As long as beauty shall enthrall.

7. *Wenn die Klänge*; text by J. von Eichendorff a 3.
   Sounds of music sweetly swelling.

8. *An's Auge des Liebsten*; text by F. Rückert à 4.
   The eyes of the lovers cling and cleave to one another.

13. *Einförmig ist der Liebe Gram*; text by Rückert à 6.
    Love ever sings the same sad song.

Other canons for women's voices not included in Op. 113 or Op. 44 are:

1. *Mir lächelt kein Frühling*; composed before 1881.
   Spring does not smile for me.

2. *O, wie sanft die Quelle*; posthumous
   O how slow the waters flow, thru the meadow winding.

3. *Grausam erweiset*, not the same of Op. 113, No. 2.

4. *Wann, wann? Wann hört der Himmel*; composed in 1885.
   When, when, O when will Heaven send protectors
   From all these autograph collectors?

Soon after Brahms became director of the *Singakademie*, a special *Brahms' Abend* was held on April 17, 1864. The women members of the chorus performed *Ave Maria*, Op. 12. Vineta, Op. 42, No. 2, was also in the programme without the other numbers of Op. 42. It seems probable, therefore, that Brahms' original setting of Vineta for four women's voices was given, rather than his arrangement of the romance for mixed voices. During the first ten years of Brahms' stay in Vienna, several performances of his compositions for women's chorus took place there and in other cities. (See Appendix G)

Except for possibly two canons, the last composition Brahms wrote for women's voices was an arrangement of Schubert's *Ellen's Zweiter Gesang*, Op. 52, No. 2 for soprano solo, chorus of sopranos, 1st and 2nd altos, accompanied by four horns and two bassoons. It was performed at a *Gesellschaft* concert on March 23, 1873. The text is Ellen's second song in Scott's poem "Lady of the Lake".

> Huntsman rest! Thy chase is done
> While our slumbrous spells assail ye,
> Dream not, with the rising sun,
> Bugles here will sound reveille.

Sleep, the deer is in his den
Sleep, thy hounds are by thee lying
Sleep nor dream in yonder glen
How thy gallant steed lay dying.

Brahms' enthusiasm for wind instruments as suitable accompaniment for women's voices is quite remarkable. One of his very early compositions, dated 1856, was the canon *Spruch* for soprano and horn. At that time, Brahms probably played the horn himself, taught by his father, but who sang the soprano part? In 1860, he wrote Op. 17, Four Songs with Harp and Horns, and finally, about 1873, he composed the setting for "The Lady of the Lake". He must have found fascination in the combination of sounds.

Taken as a whole, Brahms' choral works for women excel, in both volume and in significance for the singers, those of other nineteenth century composers. Brahms offered a greater number of compositions to women's choruses than Schubert or Schumann, more even than the prolific Gustav Holst of the twentieth century.

Into the choral literature for women which was rapidly developing "in pari passu" with the choruses themselves, Brahms incorporated a reform made necessary by some of the followers of Mendelssohn with their sentimental and insipid style. Brahms had strong romantic tendencies but he avoided the danger of sentimentality by mixing his romanticism with the austerity of the old masters of polyphony. His major works for women are remarkable for the compelling way in which the classic style merges with the romantic.

Then, too, he forged ahead of his contemporaries by providing women with choral music that is related to their experiences and at the same time has religious import.

Brahms generally, although not always, selected texts which gave women the feeling that they were in an active relation to life. The religious music has this quality, especially the *Ave Maria*, which is like a tableau, or a little drama. The women answer each other in antiphonal choirs, as if different groups of worshippers were in reality approaching the image of the Virgin. As they make their eternal invocation *Ora pro nobis*: "Pray for us", the singers are themselves the suppliants.

For the secular music, Brahms depended upon folksongs and upon the Romantic poets who derived their basic material from our rich heritage of myth and legend in which women had played an important part. In folklore, many work songs, lullabies, love songs, wedding songs, and dirges are created by women and imitations or accounts of women workers, lovers, brides, mothers, and mourners fill the poetry of nineteenth century men. The Dirge for Trenar, Op. 17, No. 4, was a particularly appropriate choice of text for a women's chorus, since dirges form the largest group of women's songs, partly because of the ancient belief that women brought about the rebirth by wailing and singing. Brahms' treatment of the chorus and instruments was the very antithesis of the eighteenth and nineteenth century conception of female choral singing. Instead of the dulcet tones of repressed young misses in a drawing-room, the music calls for the harsh, deep sounds of mature women expressing grief in an attitude that has been a religion with women since the dawn of history.

Some of the biographers intimate that Brahms placed no importance upon the music he wrote for the women's choruses but that he used the compositions merely as studies for larger works. If Brahms had published *none* of his compositions for women's chorus, this suggestion might have value. He did, however, publish opuses 12, 17, 27, 37, 44.

and 113, which are complete in themselves, beautiful and satisfactory. All of Brahms' biographers agree that he released no music that he regarded as unimportant or with which he was not thoroughly satisfied.

Everybody recognized Brahms' craving for perfection in his art and an appealing example of this characteristic of his has come from Kurt Sauermann, Friedchen Wagner's son. When Kurt was about 11 years old, his mother took him to hear Brahms conduct his 3rd Symphony at the Philharmonic Concert in Hamburg. After the concert, Kurt and his mother waited outside to congratulate Brahms.

"How did it go?" asked Brahms.

"Oh, fine!" was the boyish answer.

And then Brahms said:

"But it must become still better, must it not, still better?"

APPENDICES

A - Lists of music contained in the *Stimmenhefte*.

B - The other compositions for women's chorus.

C - List of the poets.

D - Editions of Brahms' compositions for women in the Drinker Choral Library.

E - Lists of the Brahms' manuscripts in the *Stimmenhefte*.

F - Names of some of the members of Grimm's chorus in Göttingen.

G - Dates of the composition, first publication, and some of the performances in Brahms' lifetime of his music for women's chorus.

H - References and Index.

Appendix A

List of Music in the *Stimmenhefte*

I. Twenty-five compositions for women's chorus subsequently published.

1. Op. 12 *Ave Maria* for S.S.A.A. with organ or instrumental accompaniment. (strings, two flutes, two oboes, two clarinets, two bassoons, two horns.) (see index.)

The *Ave Maria*, or Hail Mary, as an accepted devotional formula, cannot be traced before about 1050. It occurred in the Little Office, or Cursus, of the Blessed Virgin Mary which just at that time was coming into favor among the monastic orders. The words, however, are found in a Syriac ritual, 513, and also in the Liber Antiphonarius of St. Gregory the Great as the offertory of the Mass for the 4th Sunday of Advent. The first verse consists of the salutation of the angel Gabriel, Luke I-28:

Hail Mary, full of grace, the Lord is with thee.
Blessed art thou among women.

The second part is taken from the greeting of Elizabeth, Luke I-42:

And blessed the fruit of thy womb, Jesus.

The third sentence is stated by the catechism of the Council of Trent to have been framed by the Church:

Holy Mary, Mother of God, pray for us sinners now and at the hour of our death. Amen.

The official recognition of the *Ave Maria* in its complete form was finally given in the Roman Breviary, 1568.

2. Op. 17 Songs with horns and harp for S.S.A.

    1. *Es tönt ein voller Harfenklang* (see p. 50)

    2. *Komm herbei, Tod* (see p. 50)
        from Shakespeare's "Twelfth Night", Act II,
        Scene 4. The German translator was A.W. Schlegel.

    3. *Der Gärtner* (see p. 50)

    4. *Gesang aus Fingal* (see p. 50)
        "Fingal" was the name of a song cycle supposed to
        have been composed by one Ossian, an Irish hero
        of the third century. The Gaelic material, the
        bulk of which was collected in the eleventh
        century, appealed to James MacPherson (1736-96).
        He was among the first to utilize old verses for
        his own purposes. Writing in English about
        Ossian and his companions, he claimed to have
        translated portions of the Gaelic epic and pro-
        duced his work as original. The *Gesang aus Fingal*
        is a dirge for Trenar, the lover of the maiden of
        Inistore. The name of the German translator is
        unknown.

3. Op. 37 Sacred Choruses for S.S.A.A. (see p. 19)

    1. *O Bone Jesu*

        An old ecclesiastical form of prayer, derived
        from the Bible text of Luke XVII, 13, "Jesus,
        Master, have mercy on us"; and of I Peter I, 19,
        "But with the precious blood of Christ, as of a
        lamb without blemish and without spot."

    2. *Adoramus*

        A versicle and antiphon from the Roman Breviary
        for the festival of the discovery of the Holy
        Cross, celebrated on May 3.

We adore thee, Christ, and we bless Thee, for through Thy Holy Cross, Thou hast redeemed the world. Thou, who suffered for us, have pity upon us, Lord.

4. Op. 44 Twelve Songs and Romances for S.S.A.A. and piano *ad lib*. (see p. 63-65)

  1. *Minnelied (Der Holdseligen Sonder Wank)*
  2. *Der Bräutigam*
  3. *Barcarole*
  4. *Fragen*
  5. *Die Müllerin*
  6. *Die Nonne*
  7. *Nun stehen die Rosen*
  8. *Die Berge sind spitz*
  9. *Am Wildbach*
  10. *Und gehst du über den Kirchhof*
  11. *Die Braut* (see below)
  12. *Märznacht*

William Müller, author of *Die Braut*, made the following interesting notes on his poem. There was an old custom in the Rügen peninsula, surviving from matriarchal times. A daughter was allowed to inherit property and was also allowed the privilege of choosing her own husband. When she was ready to marry, she would hang an apron from her window. At this sign, all the marriageable young men would file past her house to be inspected. The bride announced her choice by sending the young man a silken scarf and he gave his consent by accepting the gift. In the case of the bride in this poem, her lover was drowned. She tells her mother that the blue apron (the color blue being a symbol of the sky goddess) she was about to hang out will be faded white by her tears. Instead of rejoicing as a bride she must mourn as a widow and sit, bowed with grief, in the special place assigned to widows in the church. (see Ophüls p. 488)

5. Op. 113 Thirteen Canons (see p. 120)

   1. *Göttlicher Morpheus à 4*
   2. *Grausam erweiset à 3*
   8. *Ein Gems auf dem Stein à 4*
   10. *Leise Töne der Brust à 4*
   11. *Ich weiss nicht, was im Hain die Taube girret à 4*
   12. *Wenn Kummer hätte zu tödten à 3*

   Psalm 13, Op. 27, is the only published composition missing in the *Stimmenhefte*. It must have been in another book, not yet located. (see p. 28 and 45)

II. Seven original songs, here for women's voices, which were subsequently arranged by Brahms for mixed chorus or for solo voice with piano.

   1. *Todtenklage* or *In stiller nacht* for S.S.A. and S.S.A.A. (*Deutsche Volkslieder für vierstimmige Chor* No. 8) (49 *Deutsche Volkslieder* No. 42)

      Those women's choruses which now sing an arrangement from the version for mixed voices should look to the original settings for women. For many years Brahms passed his composition off as a folksong. Later in his life, he conceded that the melody was his own. The poem is attributed to the Jesuit poet Spee.

   2. *Vineta* (Op. 42, No. 2) for S.S.A.A. (see p. 52)

3. *Sonntag: So hab ich doch die ganze Woche* (Op. 47 No. 3) for S.S.A.

4. *Es geht ein Wehen* (Op. 62 No. 6) for S.S.A.A. (see p. 66)

5. *Vergangen ist mir Glück und Heil* (Op. 48 No. 6) (Op. 62 No. 7) for S.S.A.A.

6. *Der Gang zum Liebchen; Es glänzt der Mond* (Op. 48 No. 1) (Op. 31 No. 3) for S.S.A.A.

7. *Maria's Kirchgang* (Op. 22 No. 2) for S.S.A.A. (see p. 21)

This *Marienlied* poem is in Kretschmer-Zuccalmaglio II, 47 (see bibliography) and in F. L. Mittler's *Deutsche Volkslieder*, p. 308 (Leipsig 1855)

The other *Marienlieder* (poems) known to have been sung by the *Hamburger Frauenchor* but not written in any of the *Stimmenhefte* at hand, may be found in the following books:

Der Englische Gruss in Kretschmer II 268 and Mittler 292.

Der Jäger in Des Knaben Wunderhorn by A. von Arnim and C. Brentano (Heidelberg 1806) and in Mittler p. 292.

Ruf Zu Maria in Mittler p. 297; in F. M. Böhme's *Altdeutsches Liederbuch* No. 591 (Leipsig 1877).

Mary Magdalene in L. Uhland's *Alte hoch und nieder deutsche Volkslieder* p. 846 (Stuttgart 1845), and in Wackernagel's *Das deutsche Kirchenlied* p. 75 (Stuttgart 1841).

Maria's Lob in Kretschmer-Zuccalmaglio II, 270.

III.   One original part song for women's voices, arranged by Brahms from a solo song previously composed.

   Mein Schatz ist nicht da (Op. 14, No. 8) for S.S.A. and S.S.A.A. (see p. 71).

IV.   One original part song for women's voices, transposed by Brahms from his setting for men's voices.

   Ich schwing mein Horn (Op. 41, No. 1) for S.S.A.A.

In Friedchen's notebook, there is written in her handwriting under the 1st soprano part for this song: "original version for four men's voices". The only men's chorus, with which we know that Brahms had anything to do before 1859, was one which he had conducted at Winsen in 1847, when he was 14 years old.· For this chorus, he wrote several pieces and probably this one. If this supposition be correct, this is the earliest composition by Brahms that we have. The song is in the style of the a capella period and the old melody with the words, dates back to 1519. Friedländer says that the song is allegorical, having been written by Duke Ulrich of Württemberg, a mighty hunter, apropos of his not being permitted to marry his love, the Countess Elisabeth of Brandenburg, but instead the far from lovely Sabina, niece of the Emperor Maximilian; Sabina being the hare in the song.

V.   Two canons not published in Brahms' lifetime.

   1.   *Töne lindernder Klang* for S.S.A.A. in G minor (see p. 73)

   2.   *Grausam erweiset* for S.S.A.A. (not the same as Op. 113) (See Appendix D)

VI.   A short original part song, not published in Brahms' lifetime.

   Dein Herzlein mild (not the same as Op. 62)   (See Appendix D)

VII. Two unfinished compositions.

    1. *Brautgesang* (accompaniment lacking)

    2. *Benedictus* (probably without accompaniment. See Chap. III) A facsimile of the *Benedictus* for S.S.A.T. can be seen in Heineman's collection, New York City.

VIII. 55 Folksongs

Title	First Line	Voice Parts
1. *Abschiedslied*	*Ich fahr dahin*	3
2. *Ade von hinnen*		2nd voice only
3. *Altes Liebeslied*	*Mein Herzlein thut mir gar so weh*	3 & 4
4. *Altes Lied*	*Mein feines Lieb*	3
5. *Das Lied vom eifersüchtigen Knaben*	*Es stehen drei Sterne am Himmel*	4
6. *Dauernde Liebe*	*Mein Schatz ich hab' es erfahren*	4
7. *Der Baum*	*Es steht ein Baum im Odenwald*	3
8. *Der Bucklichte Fiedler*	*Es wohnet ein Fiedler*	3
9. *Der Gottesacker*	*Wie sie so sanft ruhen*	3
10. *Der Jäger*	*Bei nächtlicher Weil*	4
11. *Der Ritt zum Kloster*	*Ich stand auf hohem Berge*	3
12. *Der Ritter und die Feine (MS)*	*Es stunden drei Rosen auf einem zweig*	3
13. *Der todte Gast*	*Es pochet ein Knabe*	3
14. *Der Traum (MS)*	*Ich hab' die nacht geträumet*	3
15. *Der verstellte Räuber*	*Es ritt ein Reiter wohl durch das Ried*	4
16. *Der Zimmergesell*	*Es war einmal*	3

36.	*Lied der Geisselbrüder (MS)*	*Es ging sich unsre Fraue*	4
	Mein g'muth ist mir verwirret	see under Hasler (next section)	
37.	*Mein Schatz ist auf die Wanderschaft hin*		4
38.	*Minnelied*	*Ach, bin inniglich immer*	
39.	*Minnelied or Altes Lied*	*So will ich frisch und fröhlich sein*	4
40.	*Morgen muss Ich fort von hier*		3
41.	*Pfaffenschlich (MS)*	*Der Graf stand oben*	
42.	*Scheiden*	*Ach Gott, wie weh*	4
43.	*Scheiden*	*Sind wir geschieden*	4
44.	*Schifferlied*	*Dort in den Weiden*	3 & 4
45.	*Schnitter Tod*	*Es ist ein Schnitter*	4
46.	*Schwäbische Volkslied*		3
47.	*Schwesterlein, Schwesterlein (MS)*		3
48.	*Spannung*	*Guten Abend*	4
49.	*Ständchen*	*Wach auf, mein's Herzen's Schöne*	4
50.	*Tageweis' von einer schöner Frauen*	*Wach auf, mein Hort*	4
51.	*Trennung*	*Da unten im Tale*	3
52.	*Verstohlen geht der Mond auf*		4
53.	*Vor dem Fenster*	*Soll sich der Mond*	4
54.	*Wenn ich ein Vöglein wäre (MS)*		3
55.	*Zu Strassburg auf der Schanz*		4

The German words to most of the folksongs can be found in *Kretschmer-Zuccalmaglio*.

Nos. 3, 13, 14, 26, 35, 39, and 48 of my list have been published. (see Appendix D)

Nos. 1, 3, 6, 8, 10, 11, 16, 17, 20, 28, 30, 31, 32, 33, 37, 40, 42, 43, 47, 49, 50, 53 and 55 of my list have been transcribed from the *Stimmenhefte* and are now in our library with the other material which came from Germany.

Nos. 3, 4, 5, 7, 14, 18, 20, 31, 32, 35, 37, 40, 43 and 55 of my list were used only for women's voices and not in any other setting. No significance, however, can be attached to the fact, since they are not distinguished from the other songs by any characteristic of being more suitable for women than for other groups.

The song *Verstohlen geht der Mond auf* is noteworthy on account of the fact that Brahms used the melody in his Sonata, Op. 1, and placed it as the last in his final version of the 49 Folksongs, published in 1894. It was certainly one of his favorites. He gave it to his love, Agathe, to sing and he set it in three parts for the *Hamburger Frauenchor*.

Verstohlen geht der Mond auf has an interesting history both from the point of view of women's fertility rites and of musicology. [47] Similar verses had long been sung by women who dressed flax. They stood in rows in front of the flails in order to begin the threshing. Then they sang:

> *"Wo geht sich denn der Mond auf?*
> *Blau, blau Blümelein!*
> *Obern Lindenbaum da geht er auf.*
> *Blumen im Tal,*
> *Mädchen im Saal,*
> *O, du tapfre Rosa!"*

Where, then does the moon rose?
   Blue, blue little flower!
It mounts over the Linden tree
   Rose in the dale,
Maid in the vale,
O, fairest Rosa.

The verse was repeated as many times as there were women present and the dwelling place of each one was indicated as the rising place of the moon. [48] This singing game was originally a women's rite for prosperity and luck in their work. The allusion to the moon places it definitely in the category of ritual. Folklore of all peoples brings the moon's cycle and women into accord and associates blooming flowers with girls, never with boys. But

   "Wo geht sich denn der Mond auf,
   Obern Lindenbaum da geht er auf."

is not precisely the same as:

   "Verstohlen geht der Mond auf,
   durch Silberwölkchen führt sein Lauf."

The poet-musician A. W. von Zuccalmaglio had changed it and improved it artistically, but then passed it off as a genuine folksong, calling it *Altdeutsches Minnelied*. Probably he used the original folk melody as a basis for his revised version, just as he did with the song called *Schwesterlein*.

Brahms took the song from *Deutsche Volkslieder mit ihren Original Weisen*, compiled by Zuccalmaglio and Kretschmer, the source book he used most frequently.

It is surprising to learn that, for a long time, Brahms did not discover the song to be an invention of Zuccalmaglio's and that he also used other verses composed by this ingenious

Es stunden drei Rosen in Brahms' handwriting.

man in the belief that they were real songs of the people.
In fact, of the so-called folksongs, which he set for women's
voices, only a small proportion were genuine.   These are:

> *Die Schöne Jüdin*
> *Erlaube mir, feins Mädchen*
> *Trennung (Da unten im Tale)*

The truth of the matter is that Brahms did not care whether
the music was a genuine folksong or not.   Child of his own
times, he lived when many poets and musicians made cult of
collecting folklore and using the old tales as inspiration
for art, as grist to their own mills.   Brahms followed the
fashion himself when he took Spee's poem *In Stiller Nacht*,
made his own melody and pretended it was a folksong.   His
attitude toward Zuccalmaglio was, therefore, one of tolerance
and sympathy.   It was not the exact history of every song
that had significance for him, as he showed by his lack of
interest in Ludwig Erk's monumental researches.   It was
rather the spirit in which the material was presented that
appealed to him.   Even after he knew that the "folksongs"
he had selected were contemporary compositions, he did not
discard them but merely made the comment:

> "Not really folk-music! Well, then we have one good composer
> the more." [49]

Es stunden drei Rosen is a ballad telling the story of
the Sleeping Beauty.   Friedländer attributes both the text
and the melody of this version to Zuccalmaglio.   Brahms'
musical setting is in imitation of the form used since time
immemorial by choruses of men or women when they worked or
when they entertained themselves.   The leader sang the verse
and the chorus joined in the refrain.   Brahms arranged it
first for three women's voices and later included it in his
edition of 49 Folksongs.

Solo....Three roses once grew on a single stem;
  Chorus....Fair is the summer!
Solo....A nightingale merrily sang to them;
  Chorus....Fair is the summer!
Solo....And under the blossoming rose-bush there
  Chorus....Fair is the summer!
Solo....Lay dreaming a maiden young and fair.
  Chorus....Fair is the summer!
Solo....The knight rode by where the rose-bush grew,
  Chorus....Fair is the summer!
Solo...."And what, little horse, is it startles you?"
  Chorus....Fair is the summer!
Solo...."What glimmers red in the grass and dew?"
  Chorus....Fair is the summer!
Solo...."As pink as roses of the brightest hue?"
  Chorus....Fair is the summer!
Solo....What glorious tangle does he behold?
  Chorus....Fair is the summer!
Solo....But curly locks of fine spun gold.
  Chorus....Fair is the summer!
Solo....There slept the maid so fair to see,
  Chorus....Fair is the summer!
Solo....As pure as the day she was born is she.
  Chorus....Fair is the summer!

Brahms wrote in only six of the original twenty-six
verses and omitted the part where the knight gave to Sleeping
Beauty the magic kiss which brought about the rebirth. In
many of the old legends, the text was often too crude for
19th century taste. The complete poem is printed in Ophüls'
Brahms Texte.

Since Brahms' arrangements for women's voices are not
musically outstanding, I have not attempted to give the
source of every folksong. The principal value of his other

settings lies in the beautiful piano accompaniments which is lacking in the arrangements for the *Hamburger Frauenchor*. Brahms may have improvised on the piano when he spent the evening with the girls but he definitely intended the songs for home use, for the most informal kind of amateur music making, to be sung over sewing perhaps or in the garden. Readers interested in the history of folksongs will find detailed information in Friedländer's *Brahms' Lieder*.

IX. The final category of music contained in the *Stimmenhefte* consists of thirty-two pieces by other composers, some arrangements, but most of them original. These show the repertoire of the *Hamburger Frauenchor*.

Composer	Title	Voice Parts
Bach, J. S.	Duo from Cantata 80, *Einfeste Burg*	2
	Duo from Cantata, *Gottder Herr ist Sonn und Schild*	2

These duos are for S.B., arranged for S.A.

Composer	Title	Voice Parts
Bortniansky, D.	*Vespergesang*	3
Brambach, J.	*Frühlingsglaube*	3
Byrd, Wm.	*Non nobis, Domine*	3
Caldara, A.	*Mottette: Peccavi*	3
Eccard, J.	*Marienlied: Übers' Gebirg Maria geht*	5

Brahms arranged this for women's voices from Eccard's setting for mixed voices.

Composer	Title	Voice Parts
Gallus, J.	*Passions Gesang: Ecce quo modo*	4
Händel, G. F.	Angel chorus from the Messiah	
Hasler, H. L.	*Ave Maria* (or *Liebesklage*)	
	Mein G'mut ist mir verwirret	4
Haydn, J. M.	*Heilige Nacht*	3
Kuhlau, F.	*Nachtlied* (Goethe)	4
Lorenz, C. Ad.	*Die Spröde* (Goethe)	
Lotti, A.	*Vere Languores*	3
Mendelssohn, F.	*Hebe deine Augen* (Lift thine Eyes) from Elijah	3

Title page of one of Marie Völckers' books.

Mendelssohn, F.	Recitative and chorus from St. Paul	
Mozart. W. A.	*Ave Verum* arr. by L. E. (unknown)	4
	Bei der stillen Mondes Hellen	3
Mozart, W. A.	*Der Einsamkeit (Terzett)*	
	Duet from opera Titus Ade	2
Palestrina	*Princeps Gloriosisime*	4
	Gaude Barbara Beata	4
Schumann, R.	*Wenn ich ein Vöglein ware* (from Genoveva)	3
	Tambourin Op. 69	4
	Chorus of the Houris from Paradise and The Peri	4
	Final chorus and solo from Paradise and The Peri	4
	Section from Faust	4
Sicilian Folksong	O sanctissima	3
Schalling, M.	Chorale: *Herzlich lieb hab ich*	4
Taubert, K. G. W.	*Ihr Kinder, erwacht!*	
Theriot, F.	*Am Traunsee*	bass & chorus
Witting, C.	*Frühlingsruhe*	3
Zelter, K. F.	*König von Thule*	3 & bass

The compositions by Lorenz, Taubert, and Theriot were probably not used by Brahms but belong to the repertoire of the Cuxhaven chorus. They appear only in the *Stimmenhefte* written by the Meier sisters in 1865.

On the title page of one of Marie Völcker's books are listed so many of the songs in the repertoire of the *Hamburger Frauenchor* that it seems justifiable to reproduce it. Here is the *Benedictus* and the *Brautgesang*; eight of the Romances of Op. 44; two motets of Op. 37; three numbers of the songs with harp and horns, Op. 17; four canons; *Es geht ein Wehen; Dein Herzlein mild; Ich schwing mein Horn;* Eccard's *Marien-lied*; thirty-five folksongs, including the famous *Ich fahr dahin, Innspruch,* and *Verstohlen geht der Mond auf.* Her fine, neat handwriting is still legible and is a sample of the work involved in the making of the *Stimmenhefte*.

Appendix B

The Other Compositions for Women's Voices

Op. 27   Psalm 13 for S.S.A. with organ (see pp. 28, 45)

Op. 37   No. 3   Regina coeli for S.S.A.A.

An antiphon of the Virgin Mary, sung in the Easter Festival at the end of the ecclesiastical horary prayer.

Rejoice, Queen of the Heavens, divinely blessed of women. From the dead thy Son is risen, as was promised. O pray for our Salvation.
Hallelujah!

Op. 113   Canons

Nos. 3, 4, 5, 6, 7, 9, 13 (see p. 84)

Ellen's *Zweiter Gesang* for S. solo, S.S.A. with four horns and two bassoons. (see p. 85)

Appendix C

List of Poets
(see Ophüls' *Brahms' Texte*)

Adalbert von Chamisso 1781-1838
Die Mühle Op. 44 No. 5 (vol. I of *Gesammelte Werke*)

Joseph Freiherr von Eichendorff 1788-1857
Der Gärtner Op. 17 No. 3 (from the novel *Aus dem Leben eines Taugenichts* and from *Gedichte*)

Der Bräutigam Op. 44 No. 2 (from the tragedy *Der letztte Held von Marienburg* IV, 2 and from *Gedichte*)

Ein Gems auf dem Stein Op. 113 No. 8 (from the novel *Das Schloss Dürande* and from *Gedichte*)

Wenn die Klänge Op. 113 No. 7 (from *Gedichte*, verse 3 of *Anklänge*)

Hoffman von Fallersleben 1798-1874
So lange Schönheit Op. 113 No. 6 (translated from the Greek in *Gedichte* Bd. I 249)

Johann Wolfgang von Goethe 1749-1832
Göttlicher Morpheus Op. 113 No. 1 (*Epigramme*, No. 85)

Grausam erweiset Op. 113 No. 2 (*Vier Jahreszeiten*; *Sommer* No. 19)

Anastasius Grün 1806-1876
Sagen Op. 44 No. 4 (translated from Slavic in *Volkslieder aus Krain*)

Paul Heyse 1830-1914
Nun Stehen die Rosen Op. 44 No. 7
Die Berge sind Spitz Op. 44 No. 8
Am Wildbach Op. 44 No. 9
Und gehst du über den Kirchhof Op. 44 No. 10

Dein Herzlein mild
Es geht ein Wehen Op. 62 No. 6
           (all from *Der Jungbrunnen*)

Wilhelm Müller 1794-1827
  Vineta Op. 42 No. 2 (*Gedichte*)
  Die Braut Op. 44 No. 11 (see p. 146) (*Gedichte*)

(see p. 146)

Friedrich Rückert 1788-1866
  Ich weiss nicht Op. 113 No. 11
    (No. 43 Abth I der Ital. *Gedichte* Bd. V)

  Einförmig ist der Liebe Gram Op. 113 No. 13
    (*Hafisens Lieder*, *Östliche Rosen*. *Bd. V Abth I*)

  Wenn Kummer Op. 113 No. 12 and

  An's Auge des Liebsten Op. 113 No. 9 (both translated from
    the Arabian in *Gesammelten Werken* Bd. II)

Friedrich Ruperti 1805-1867
  Es tönt ein voller Harfenklang Op. 17 No. 1
    (*Dunkles Laub*, *Jugend-Gedichte*)

Johann Ludwig Uhland 1787-1862
  Die Nonne Op. 44 No. 6   (*Gedichte*)
  Märznacht Op. 44 No. 12   (*Gedichte*)
  Frühlingsruhe   (*Gedichte*)
  Brautgesang   (*Gedichte*)

Johann Heinrich Voss 1751-1826
  Minnelied, Der Holdseligen Sonder Wank Op. 44 No. 1
    (*Oden und Lieder* No. X)

Appendix D

Edition with English words by Henry S. Drinker,
Drinker Choral Library, Westminster Choir College,
Princeton, New Jersey

1. Seven Folksongs for S.S.A. and S.S.A.A. from the Hamburg
   Stimmenhefte. U. of P. Choral Series No. 74.

   a. *Altes Lied. So will ich frisch und fröhlich seyn.*
      In happy hope my heart to-day with cheer and joy is
      ringing.

   b. *Der Todte Gast. Es pochet ein Knabe sachte.*
      A lover is gently tapping on his sweetheart's
      windowpane.

   c. *Ich hab' die Nacht geträumet.*
      At night when I was dreaming.

   d. *Altes Liebeslied. Mein Herzlein thut mir gar zu weh!*
      My soul is filled with fear and woe!

   e. *Es waren zwei Königskinder.*
      The Princess was watching the water.

   f. *Spannung. Guten Abend, guten Abend, mein täusiger
      Schatz.*
      God bless you this evening, beloved one mine.

   g. *Drei Vöglein. Mit Lust thät ich ausreiten.*
      While I was gaily riding.

2. Six *Marienlieder* for S.S.A.A. U. of P. Choral Series
   No. 75.

   a. *Der englische Gruss.* The Angel's Greeting.
      All hail to thee, Mary, thou blest among women.

   b. *Maria's Kirchgang.* When Mary went to Church.
      When Mary once to church would go.

   c. *Der Jäger.* The Hunter.
      A hunter went a'hunting.

d. *Ruf zu Maria.* Prayer to Mary.

O Mother of God, we cry to Thee.

e. *Magdelena.*

Early on that Easter morn.

f. *Maria's Lob.* Praise to Mary.

O, Mary, joy of Heaven bright.

3. Eccard's *Marienlieder.* U. of P. Choral Series No. 75a.
Uber's Gebirge Maria Geht.

Over the mountain Mary went.

4. Four Romances from Op. 44 for S.S.A.A. U. of P. Choral Series 72.

a. No. 1 *Minnelied.* Love Song.

To my darling one, strong and gay.

b. No. 3 *Barcarolle.*

O, fisher come thee hither, Fidelin.

c. No. 4 *Fragen.* Questions.

O, why have I long curly hair?

d. No. 5 *Die Müllerin.* Maid of the Mill.

The sails of the wind mill are sweeping.

5. Three Romances from Op. 44 for S.S.A.A. U. of P. Choral Series 73.

a. No. 2 *Der Bräutigam.* The Bridegroom.

From every mountain sounding.

b. No. 4 *Nun stehen die Rosen.*

The red, red roses are blooming.

c. No. 9 *Am Wildbach.*

The willows by the water are waving night and day.

6. Canon from Op. 44 for S.S.A.A. U. of P. Choral Series No. 66.

No. 12 *Märznacht.* Night in March.

Hark! The March wind is roaring!

7. Vineta for S.S.A.A. U. of P. Choral Series No. 21.
   Aus des Meeres tiefem, tiefem grunde.
   Up from out the lowest depths of ocean.

8. *Es geht ein·Wehen.* U. of P. Choral Series No. 22.
   A sigh goes floating through the wood.

9. *Todtenklage* or *In Stiller Nacht*. U. of P. Choral
   Series No. 23.
   Lament or In Dead of Night.

10. Two Canons. U. of P. Choral Series No. 25.
    Töne, lindernder Klang.
    Music, however soft.

    Grausam erweiset (not Op. 113)
    Cruel, ah cruel.

11. *Dein Herzlein mild.* (not Op. 62) U. of P. Choral
    Series No 24.
    Thou gentle Heart.

Appendix E

List of Brahms' manuscripts from the Völckers *Stimmenhefte*

1. *Der Herr erbarm sich unser.*
   "May the Lord have mercy on us!"
   This is the refrain sung by the chorus to the *Lied der Geissel brüder*, the first line of which is *Es Ging sich unsre Fraue*, "Our Lady was walking along."

2. *Die Verzauberte Nachtigall* (see p. 70)

3. *Es stunden drei Rosen* (see p. 101)

4. *Es waren zwei Königskinder* (see Drinker, U. of P. Choral Series 74)

5. *Ich hab' die Nacht geträumet* (see Drinker, U. of P. Choral Series 74)

6. *Ich hört ein Sichlein rauschen.*

7. *Mein lieb blau Blümelein; es muss geschieden sein.*
   "My lovely little blue flower, we must be parted." is the refrain sung by the chorus to a song which begins *Demm Himmel will ich klagen.*

8. *Mein Schatz ist nicht da* (see p. 71)

9. *Schwesterlein.*

10. *Töne, lindernder Klang* (see p. 73)

11. *Und was sein Versprechen (Der Graf stand oben)*
    "And his word will be broken" is the refrain to a song which begins "The Count stands up in his castle," called *Pfaffenschlich.*

12. *Wenn ich ein Vöglein wäre* (see p. 71)

Brahms probably wrote the songs down in the Völckers' *Stimmenhefte* at the rehearsal or when he was spending the evening at their house, expecting the other girls to copy the lines off another time.

Appendix F

Names of some of the women in Grimm's chorus in Göttingen

Phippine Grimm, nee Ritmüller
Agathe von Siebold, m. Carl Schütte
Josephine von Siebold, m. Gabriel Wesley Dingle, Charleston, S.C.
Helene, Emilie, and Pauline Wöhler
Fanny Wöhler, m. Karl Bargheer, Detmold
Bertha Wagner, also m. Karl Bargheer
Sophie Wagner
Hedwig Sauppe
Marianna Hasse
Mathilda Grupen, m. Philip Spitta, the Bach biographer
Emma Henrici
Elisabet Besser
Helene Zachariae
Therese Wedemeyer
   from Michelmann, *Agathe von Siebold*

Letters or diaries of these women might reveal some interesting details about the choral singing of women.

Karl Bargheer conducted the Schlosschor in Detmold.

He was a composer of merit and wrote several pieces for women's chorus. The fact that he married two of the young women who had sung in Grimm's chorus at Göttingen explains his interest in music for women's voices. Most of the choral literature for women has had its origin in this way -- by the immediate incentive of some particular group needing music.

Dates of Composition, First Publication, and Some of
the Performances in Brahms' Lifetime of his
Music for Women's Chorus.

Op. 12 *Ave Maria*

    a. Composed Göttingen, September 1858.

    b. First Publication: J. Rieter-Biedermann, 1861
       Gesamt-Ausgabe Bd. XIX.

    c. Performances:

1. *Hamburger Frauenchor*. St. Peter's Church,
June 8, 1859.

2. *Hamburger Frauenchor*. St. Peter's Church,
September 26, 1859.

It is a question whether the singing in St. Peter's Church on
September 19 should be called a performance or a rehearsal
for the performance on September 26. There were listeners
present upon the 19th, but another rehearsal was held by the
Hamburger Frauenchor on September 22 and still another on
Sunday, the 25th. Both of these were clearly in preparation
for the final concert on the 26th when the inkstand was
presented to Brahms and the season closed. In any case, the
first performance of the *Ave Maria* preceded the September
dates and took place on June 8.

3. *Hamburger Frauenchor*. Wörmer's Hall
December 2, 1859.

4. Grimm's *Frauenchor* at Göttingen, January 15, 1860.

5. Grimm's *Frauenchor* at Hanover, January 16, 1860.

6. Bernard Scholz in Hanover.

7. Brahms' *Singakademie*, Vienna, April 17, 1864 in the
hall of the *Gesellschaft der Musikfreunde*.

8. Women's Chorus at Krefeld, 1868.

Op. 17   *Four Songs with Harp and Horns*

  a. Composed Hamburg, 1860.

  b. First Published by N. Simrock, 1862. *Gesamt-Ausgabe Bd. XIX.*

  c. Performances:

1. *Hamburger Frauenchor* at Grädener's Academy, May 2, 1860. (without No. 4, Fingal)

2. *Hamburger Frauenchor* in Wörmer's Hall, January 15, 1861.

3. *Hamburger Frauenchor* at Altona, January 16, 1861.

4. Wiener *Singakademie*, April 10, 1863.

5. Ladies Choir in Basel, November 17, 1865 conducted by Direktor Reiter, Frau Reiter playing the harp.

Op. 22   *Marienlieder*

  a. Composed Hamburg, June and July 1859 (but not No. 3)

  b. First Published by J. Rieter-Biedermann, 1862, for mixed voices. *Gesamt-Ausgabe Bd. XXI.*

  c. Performances by women's voices:

1. *Hamburger Frauenchor*. St. Peter's Church, September 26, 1859. Nos. 1, 2, 4, 5.

Op. 27   *Psalm 13*

  a. Composed Hamburg, August 21, 1859.

  b. First Published by C. A. Spina, 1864. *Gesamt-Ausgabe Bd. XX.*

  c. Performances by:

1. *Hamburger Frauenchor*, St. Peter's Church, September 26, 1859.

2. *Gesellschaft der Musikfreunde*, Vienna, April 2, 1876.

3. Women's Chorus in Münster, November 9, 1878.

4. At the *Singakademie* Concert, Vienna, March 11, 1885.

Op. 37   *Three Sacred Choruses*

  a. Composed Nos. 1 and 2. Hamburg, May 1859. No. 3, Vienna, December, 1863.

b. First Published by J. Rieter-Biedermann, 1866. *Gesamt-Ausgabe Bd. XXI.*

c. Performances by:

1. *Hamburger Frauenchor*, Nos. 1 and 2, St. Peter's Church, June 8, 1859.

2. *Hamburger Frauenchor*, Nos. 1 and 2, September 26, 1859.

3. At Julie von Asten's house, No. 3, 1863.

Op. 42 *Vineta*

a. Composed Hamburg, April, 1860.

b. First Published by Fr. Cranz, 1868, for mixed chorus. *Gesamt-Ausgabe Bd. XXI.*

c. Performances by:

1. *Singakademie* (probably by the women only), April 17, 1864.

Op. 44 *Twelve Songs and Romances*

a. Composed Hamburg between 1859-1863.

b. First Published by J. Rieter-Biedermann, 1866. *Gesamt-Ausgabe Bd. XXI.*

c. Performances by:

1. *Hamburger Frauenchor*, Nos. 1 and 2, Wörmer's Hall, January 15, 1861.

2. Ladies Choir in Basel, Nos. 1, 2, 4, 10, March 4, 1869.

3. *Singakademie*, Vienna, Nos. 7, 8, 9, 10. March 11, 1885.

4. Mandyczewski Chorus, Nos. 3, 11, Vienna, February 2, 1895.

When offering Simrock the Romances for publication, Brahms wrote:

> "You know about the *frequent performances* of these songs and you have been asking for them"...

Did the von Asten group sing six numbers of Op. 44 at their private concert in April, 1863?

Op. 113 *Thirteen Canons*

  a. Composed Nos. 1, 2, 8, 10, 11, 12
      Hamburg 1859-1863.
      Date on No. 12: May 7, 1863.
      Nos. 6, 7, probably Düsseldorf, 1857-1858.
      Nos. 3, 4, 5, 9, 13, Vienna after 1863.

  b. First Published C. F. Peters, 1891. *Gesamt-Ausgabe Bd. XXI*.

  c. Performances by:

1. *Hamburger Frauenchor* in private.

2. Mandyczewski's von Hornbostel Women's Chorus at Purkersdorf, 1863.

Ellen's Zweiter Gesang

  a. Composed probably Vienna 1873.

  b. First Publication: *Deutsche Brahms Gesellschaft*, Berlin 1906. *Gesamt-Ausgabe Bd. XIX*.

  c. First Performance: *Gesellschaft Konzert*, Vienna, March 23, 1873.

While von Ehrmann's catalogue of the dates of the composition, first publication, and first performance is as complete as it is possible to make it, the list of performances of women's choral music during Brahms's lifetime is far from satisfactory.

How prevalent women's choruses were and how popular Brahms was with other conductors are both obscure subjects. Grimm's letter to Brahms in which he wrote: "With the three harp and horn songs, I cannot come to any understanding, nor some of the *Jungbrunnen Lieder* [24]....." may have reflected a widespread scepticism as to the value of Brahms' music even many years after 1860. If so good a musician and so warm a friend of Brahms' did not understand Op. 17 and Op. 44, others may not have wanted to perform them either. Let us hope that more material on this phase of amateur music will come to light.

In our own times, when women's choruses have developed so rapidly through the institutional support of public schools, colleges, and clubs, there is no doubt that Brahms' music has a large circulation. For women's choruses in the United States, the catalogue "Selected List of Choruses for Women's Voices" by Arthur W. Locke, Smith College, Northampton, Massachusetts, is invaluable. In it, every available composition by Brahms, with the name of the publisher who handles it, is entered.

Appendix H

References

1. Litzmann *Letters* July 3, 1859
2. Memoirs of Friedchen Wagner
3. *Briefwechsel IV*, p. 62
4. Litzmann *Letters*, December 20, 1858
5. *Briefwechsel IV*, pp. 76, 78, 83
6. Hübbe, p. 20
7. Kalbeck, I, 2 p. 361
8. *Briefwechsel, Simrock* 1860 September IX p. 23
9. Litzmann *Letters*, July 16, 1859
10. *Briefwechsel* - Joachim I p. 248
11. F. May, I p. 240 (aus von Meysenbug, *J. Brahms' Jugendtagen*)
12. Hübbe, p. 22; also F. May, I p. 240
13. Kalbeck, I, 2 p. 368
14. Litzmann *Letters*: also Niemann, p. 70
15. Niemann, p. 71
16. Litzmann, *Letters*
17. Litzmann, *Letters*
18. Kalbeck, I, 2 p. 396
19. Letter from Kurt Sauermann
20. Hübbe, p. 23; also F. May, I p. 241
21. *Briefwechsel*, IV, p. 90
22. *Briefwechsel*, Joachim I, p. 258
23. Litzmann, *Letters*
24. *Briefwechsel*, IV, p. 92 and 103
25. Litzmann *Letters*, March 3rd, 1860
26. Litzmann *Letters*, April 2, 1860
27. *Briefwechsel*, Joachim I, p. 270
28. Litzmann *Letters*
29. German edition of the Avertimento: F. May, App. to Vol I; also Kalbeck, I, 2 p. 407

30. Hübbe, p. 67

31. *Briefwechsel*, IV, p. 101

32. Litzmann, *Clara Schumann* II, p. 181

33. Hübbe, p. 32

34. Elise Brahms' Letters, December 20, 1862. See Geiringer.

35. *Briefwechsel*, Joachim I, p. 286

36. *Briefwechsel*, IV, p. 101

37. *Briefwechsel*, Joachim I, pp. 288, 309

38. Litzmann, *Clara Schumann*, II p. 189

39. Litzmann, *Clara Schumann*, Paris, April 27, 1862. II p. 207

40. Kalbeck, I, 2 p. 442

41. Kalbeck, I, 2 p. 442

42. F. May, II, p. 31; also Friedländer, p. 210

43. Geiringer, *Correspondence of Brahms and Mandyczewski*, p. 345

44. Kalbeck, IV, 1, p. 221

45. Kalbeck, IV, 1, p. 220

46. Kalbeck, IV, 1, p. 220

47. For songs attributed to women, see Drinker, *Music and Women* Chap. I, II, III

48. Friedländer, p. 249 (refers to an article in the *Kolnische Zeitung*, December 5, 1847, entitled *Volksfeste und altertümliche Volksbräuche Zwischen Wupper un Sieg* and another article in *Das festliche Jahr* by Otto Freiherr von Reinsberg-Düringsfeld p. 351, Leipsig, 2nd edition)

49. Friedländer, p. 203, note 1

INDEX